Bridge to Excellence

Building Capacity for
Sustainable Performance

Shawn M. Galloway

SCE Press

ISBN: 979-8-9873873-1-3

For Terry L. Mathis, my mentor, business partner and friend.

Contents

Contents

Introduction

The bridge I'll be discussing in this book was originally conceived of as a Bridge to Safety Excellence in 2008 by my retired business partner, Terry Mathis. Specifically, it was designed to help leaders achieve and repeat great results; know precisely what is creating the results; develop confidence in the system capacity to prevent undesirable outcomes and to recover when they do occur; and to create an organizational culture dedicated to this pursuit, with a shared mindset that, regardless of how well we are performing, continuous improvement is always possible.

I am passionate about helping leaders achieve excellence in their safety performance and culture. But the more I spoke with leaders about the Bridge and helped them implement it for their organizations, the clearer it became that this was not just a pathway to pursuing excellence in occupational safety. Leaders at all levels realized that the Bridge concept could be applied to production, human resources, sales, and more; to departments and units and plants; to teams and one-on-one associations; to relationships between leadership, management, and workers; to just about everything having to do with an organization and its operations. Most crucially, it could be used to enhance the organization's ability to thrive in a competitive, ever-changing, and always challenging world.

Thus, now I speak of the Bridge as a Bridge to Excellence, specifically to *sustained* excellence (see Diagram 1). As you'll see, every organization has a Bridge, whether they know it or not, utilize it or not. The question is, does their Bridge take them across the roiling rivers of competition, technological change, evolving customer preferences, workforce changes, supply chain disruptions, pandemics, regulation, and more? Does it carry them over all of this to their goal of sustained excellence? Or does it take them somewhere else?

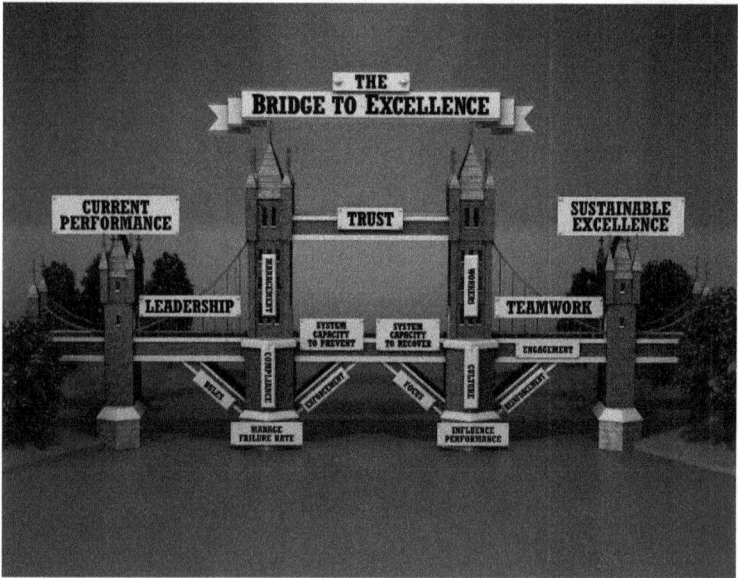

Diagram 1: The Bridge to Excellence

Chapter One – Excellence

What is excellence?

At first glance, the answer seems obvious and brief: excellence is the ability to achieve great results.

In business we measure excellence, or the lack thereof, by tracking sales, profits, stock price, and other metrics. In war, success may be defined in terms of battles won and territory conquered. In Hollywood, excellence might be measured by tickets sold and Oscars won. And in sports, teams look to victories versus losses and records broken, among other things.

Excellence can't always be counted and calculated with double decimal point precision; some things are not easily converted to firm numbers, including workers' trust in management and the degree to which a particular team is working together. Still, we all have a good idea of what excellence means. It means winning, exceeding the metrics, grabbing the brass ring, being the industry leader, or something similar.

Of course, being excellent today doesn't guarantee that you'll always be so. General Robert E. Lee of the Confederate States of America chalked up a series of impressive battlefield victories in 1862 and 1863 but was unable to repeat his success after that. He was forced to surrender in 1865, effectively ending the American Civil War. There are many similar stories in business. Blockbuster "owned" the video rental sector in the 1990s and early 2000s but was trampled underfoot by Netflix. Similarly, Toys "R" Us, Borders Books, Pier 1 Imports, and many other formerly familiar names went from being purveyors of excellence to entries on "remember them?" lists.

So, we need to expand our definition of excellence to capture the idea that it must be extended over time: excellence is the ability to achieve *and repeat* great results, to continue grabbing the brass ring, day after day, month after month, year after year.

Die-hard basketball fans know that the UCLA Bruins college basketball team was practically unbeatable in the 1960s and early '70s. The Bruins had perfect records—30 wins and 0 losses—in 1964, 1967, 1972, and 1973. In 1968, 1969, and 1971, they were 29-1. In 1965 and 1970, they were "only" 28-2. And they won ten national championships during that run of repeated excellence. Pennsylvania Railroad achieved and repeated great results year after year from about 1870 to 1920, as did General Motors from 1925 to 1975 and IBM from 1930 to 1980. The Beatles poured out hit song after hit song until they disbanded. Perhaps the most impressive run of repeated excellence has been New Zealand's national rugby team, the All Blacks. They have, since 1903, won over seventy-five percent of their games. That's more than a century of top-flight play!

In business, one measure of success is to have your company's stock included in the Dow Jones Industrial Average. This is a matter of great pride for the blue chippers included, for it indicates an ability to achieve and repeat results that place them in the top ranks. But for every company like General Electric, Bethlehem Steel, and

Sears, which were on the list decade after decade, there are companies like Webvan, which not only failed to be listed on the Dow Jones but went from IPO to bankruptcy in less than two years. Pets.com made the same "journey of un-excellence" in only nine months.

Webvan and Pets.com are extreme examples, but the reality is that relatively few businesses (or other organizations) achieve and repeat great results over long periods of time. Today, the average lifespan of a company listed on the S&P 500 is only about twenty years, much less than the sixty-year lifespan typical in the 1950s.[1] There are many reasons for this, including the rapid advance of technology over the past couple of decades. And the disruptions caused by COVID-19 have yet to settle, while those created by the volatile sociopolitical situation in the United States have yet to be fully defined, let alone understood.

The fact that we live in an era defined by technology, turnover, and tumult means that you can't just achieve and repeat great results: *you have to know how you are doing so*. Success should not be an accident, because if it is, you won't be able to repeat it. A pharmaceutical company, for example, may combine ingredients and come up with a great new medicine, worth tens or hundreds of millions of dollars, but if they don't understand the sciences underlying pharmaceutical

---

[1] Michael Sheetz, "Technology Killing off Corporate America: Average Life Span of Companies under 20 Years," *CNBC*, updated August 24, 2017, https://www.cnbc.com/2017/08/24/technology-killing-off-corporations-average-lifespan-of-company-under-20-years.html.

development and the various forces influencing sales, each new attempt will be a shot in the dark—and a very expensive one, at that.

Relying on luck is not a good strategy. You have to know why you are successful. You have to identify and understand all the internal pressures within your organization and truly understand how you fit into the external environment in which you operate. You have to understand the way in which that environment is evolving and how you might alter your operation in response so that you will continue to get and repeat great results.

It was no accident that the UCLA college basketball team was practically unbeatable during its run of excellence. Their coach, John Wooden, carefully considered why his teams were winning, devised principles of success, and made sure they were followed to the letter. His approach even included teaching his players how to put their shoes and socks on so they wouldn't develop blisters that would prevent them from playing. When training commenced each year, Wooden carefully demonstrated how to put socks on, pulling them tight to eliminate wrinkles, and how to tie basketball shoes so they would fit snugly and not slide across the foot. You may snicker at the idea of teaching college students how to put their shoes and socks on, but Wooden knew why he was able to achieve and repeat success year after year, and he made sure his players knew it too. So, the definition of excellence now has two parts. Excellence is (1) the ability to achieve and repeat great results and (2) knowing precisely how you achieved those results.

Can Excellence Survive the Unexpected Disaster?

If you can achieve and repeat great results, knowing precisely how you did so, your organization will be excellent. You may not "win" every single quarter or year or game or season or campaign, but you will regularly exceed the metrics, score the most points, sell the most tickets, capture the most territory, or do whatever is considered excellent in your arena. But then, every so often, something will go wrong. It is inevitable: something *will* go terribly wrong.

It happened recently to the justice system in Los Angeles when the man suspected of shooting Lady Gaga's dogwalker walked out of prison. He didn't bust out or tunnel out. He wasn't granted bail or found innocent at trial. Instead, a simple clerical error allowed a man being held on charges of attempted murder to be walked to the door and let loose.

It happened to American Airlines and United Airlines, whose airplanes were hijacked and used to terrible effect on 9/11.

It happened to Yahoo, Equifax, Marriott International, Facebook, Target, the US Office of Personnel Management, LinkedIn, Adobe, First American Financial Corporation, and other major organizations, all of whom have suffered major data breaches over the past decade or so.

It happened to the producers of the movie *All the Money in the World* when their star, Kevin Spacey, was accused of sexual misconduct and they could not release the movie with him in it.

It happened to Watson Grinding and Manufacturing in 2019, when an explosion in one of their buildings, just a few miles from my home, killed three people and heavily damaged numerous nearby homes.

It happened to Martha Stewart Living Omnimedia, when it's CEO and chief "product," Martha Stewart, was found guilty of conspiracy and other charges in the ImClone stock case and locked up in federal prison.

It happened to the US Navy when one of its submarines, the very high-tech Greenville, accidently struck and sunk a fishery training boat filled with teenagers, killing nine.

It happened to Southwest Airlines in 2021, when the company was forced to ground every single one of its airplanes, all across the country.

My point is not to criticize but to highlight the fact that bad things can and do happen. That's why following all the rules isn't enough to ensure that you can achieve and repeat great results. You must also be prepared to deal with the unthinkable, even when you can't imagine what that terrible thing might be. The terrible unimaginable is difficult to anticipate because such disasters aren't usually triggered by a single error or omission. Instead, they may be caused by a series of errors or omissions that come together in just the right way to create just the wrong outcome, which makes them so difficult to predict. But you must be able to recover, or your organization will fall into chaos and possibly collapse.

So, we must extend the definition of excellence to include the ability to handle the hazards and risks of your work, both known and unknown. That is, you must create the ability to prevent and recover from bad events, predictable and unpredictable.

It is possible to prepare for unknown hazards, even if you can't imagine what they might be. For example, during NASA's space shuttle program, the shuttles carried extra fuel in case something went wrong on reentry. With extra fuel in its tanks, a shuttle had the capacity to go around and try again. NASA engineers knew they could not predict and prevent everything that might go wrong in space, so they built in the ability to fail and recover.

Like NASA, you must build in systems to deal with unknown hazards in your operations, whatever they may be. You can't assume that since you've done everything that you are supposed to do, there will be no problems. It doesn't matter how many laws, rules, and regulations you follow. It doesn't matter how many onsite surveys you have conducted and seminars you have run. You must be prepared to recover from events you cannot predict and prevent.

Our definition of excellence now has three parts. Excellence is (1) the ability to achieve and repeat great results, (2) knowing precisely how you achieved those results, and (3) building into your systems the capacity to deal with and recover from exposure to hazards and risks.

The Fourth and Final Point

Compaq Computers was well satisfied with its position in the computer industry. So was Polaroid, which dominated the instant camera sector. They, like many other organizations, believed they were as good as could be. They were convinced they had achieved enduring excellence, yet they're gone.

Some of the companies I work with are not so certain that they have addressed all the issues within the organization that need attention, not sure that they have solved all their problems. So, they create a "someday" file, where they put issues they know they need to deal with but don't know how to today. They pull that file out every so often and review it, for they understand that a solution may pop up as new discoveries occur, new people with new ideas join the firm, or maybe enough people who were comfortable with the status quo have retired or otherwise left the organization.

In other words, they maintain the mindset that they can always be better. With respect to safety, for example, they're not satisfied at having reduced the "near miss" or "days lost to injury" metrics. They understand that the absence of injury is not the same as developing enduring safety excellence. In finance, they're not satisfied at having gone X number of years without an IRS audit. In customer service, they're not popping corks because customer review ratings haven't dropped over the past three years.

In other words, they don't tell themselves that because nothing bad has happened for a while, everything must be great. Instead, they maintain the mindset that they can always be better. They look to create sustainable excellence that will carry them through time, over the inevitable blips, goofs, and absolute disasters they know will occur. You can see this in organizations that deliberately do not talk about "best practices," for they know that doing so can blind them to the fact that they can always be better. Instead, they talk about "better practices," a phrase which reminds them that, although they have improved, they can strive to be even better. When working with Cintas, I learned about their attitude of "positive discontent," which is, "We're never satisfied with the status quo or content to leave things as they are. We're always seeking improvements to our processes, systems, products, and services."

Thus, the definition of excellence—sustainable excellence—needs to be extended to include the idea that we can always be better. Thus, excellence is (1) the ability to achieve and repeat great results, (2) knowing precisely how you achieved those results, (3) building into your systems the capacity to deal with and recover from exposure to hazards and risks, and (4) maintaining a mindset that you can always be better, regardless of how well you're currently performing.

No organization has ever been excellent at all things at all times. They've all had their ups and downs. They've all been caught by surprise or have been over-confident at points. And some organizations that aren't excellent at all manage to soldier on, if only because they lack significant competition or because they are so large it takes them a long time to die. But if you're looking to build long-lasting success in a competitive, cutthroat, interlinked, ever-changing world, your first metric should be this: How are we doing on the road to excellence, to excellence we can sustain over time and through the blips, goofs, and absolute disasters that we know lie in our future?

Key Points about Excellence

- Excellence is the ability to achieve and repeat great results, knowing precisely how you achieved those results, building into your systems the capacity to deal with and recover from exposure to hazards and risks, and maintaining a mindset that you can always be better, regardless of how well you're currently performing.
- Being excellent today doesn't guarantee that you'll always be so.
- Success should not be an accident, because if it is, you won't be able to repeat it.
- The unimaginable problem is often caused by a series of errors or omissions that come together in just the right way to create just the wrong outcome, which makes it so difficult to predict.
- Maintaining a "someday" file, where you place issues you are unable to deal with today, allows you to review them occasionally and possibly address them in the future.

Questions to Consider

1. How is excellence defined in your organization?
2. On a scale of one to ten, with one indicating you have yet to begin and ten that you are there, what score would you give your organization for achieving excellence as you define it?
3. On the same scale of one to ten, what score would others in your organization give to the previous question?

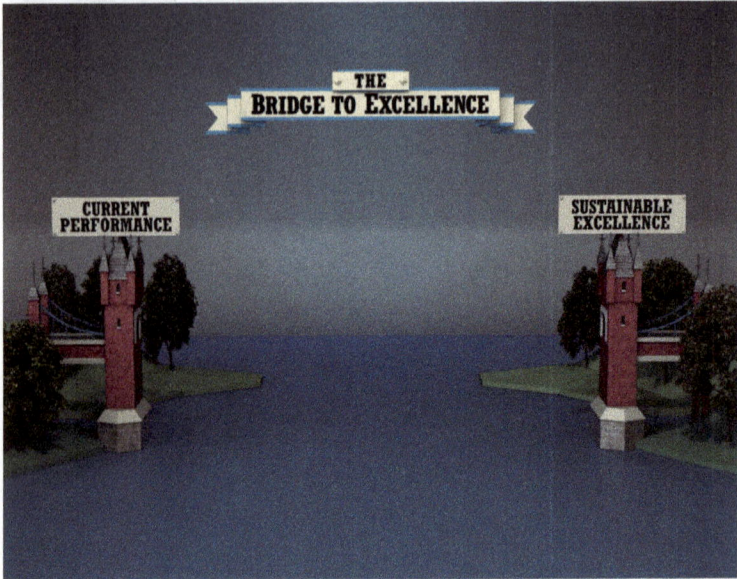

Diagram 2: Current Performance and Sustainable Excellence

When speaking of achieving excellence I use the metaphor of a bridge, specifically, a Bridge to Excellence that takes you from where you are now to where you want to be, from your Current Performance to Sustainable Excellence.

Think of Current Performance and Sustainable Excellence as being two banks of a deep and wide river that races along with sometimes frightening force (see Diagram 2. And think of the river's waters as being the flood of regulations your organization must deal with, your competition, the difficulty of hiring and retaining personnel, changing customer tastes, supply chain disruptions, pandemics, and more.

You can't swim or row across this roiling river, and you certainly cannot leap from one side to the other. The only way to move from Current Performance—which may be less than you want it to be—to Sustainable Excellence is to build a bridge from one side of the river to the other. The bridge must be strong to withstand powerful water and wind forces, but also flexible to bend a bit when the waters or winds rise or when earthquakes or tornados strike. It must be structurally complex enough to accommodate all the necessary components, yet simple enough that everyone involved can understand it and help build and maintain it.

Think about how you would build a Bridge to Excellence for your organization. The bridge's road, or deck, must be laid across pillars rising up from the water, so you begin by building at least one pillar. This initial pillar has to be the Compliance Pillar, which represents all the legal things necessary to start and run your organization. Whether it's an international corporation, a local business, political action committee, chamber of commerce, church, or charitable foundation, or what have you, you must comply with various laws, rules, and regulations. You must have licenses and permits. You must have bathrooms and scheduled breaks for employees, OSHA signs posted in the appropriate places, handrails on staircases, and so on. If your organization is a restaurant you must comply with federal, state, and local regulations concerning food safety. If it's an airline, you must comply with American and possibly international regulations having to do with passenger safety and airplane inspection and maintenance. No matter the nature of your organization, even if it's a tiny hamburger stand, you must have a Compliance Pillar just to remain open.

You must also have a Management Tower. After all, somebody has to make sure everyone is following the laws and regulations, which can be complex, contradictory, and so numerous that no one can know them all. Since the very first job of management is to make sure the organization is in compliance or else it be closed down, the Management Tower sits atop the Compliance Pillar.

To be certain you remain in compliance, you secure the bridge's deck to the Compliance Pillar with a strut called Rules. That is, management devises a series of rules to make sure the workforce is in compliance. On a factory floor, these rules might have to do with wearing personal protective equipment, following "lock out, tag out" procedures when working on energized equipment, performing lifts in the prescribed manner, and so on. In office areas, rules might include making sure that all communication goes through company computers and that certain documents are either archived or shredded. In food preparation and service areas, rules might include making sure refrigeration and heating units are available and at the right temperature.

Management is very eager to make sure that the rules are followed, so it adds an additional piece to the Bridge, called the Enforcement Strut, opposite the Rules

Strut. Some organizations attempt to enforce compliance by coming down hard on those who break the rules, while others prefer to coach errant workers and reward those who carefully follow the rules. We'll talk more about rules and enforcement in the chapters to come.

Extending the "Halfway Bridge"

Now you have the first part of your Bridge to Excellence: compliance, management, rules, and enforcement. Unfortunately, as you'll notice in diagram 3 this halfway bridge doesn't take you very far. It ends abruptly over the river, halfway to Sustainable Excellence.

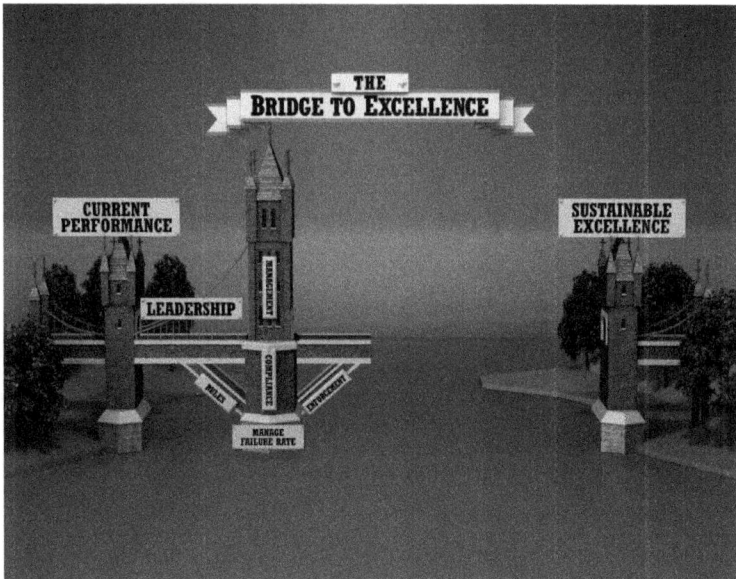

Diagram 3: Compliance, Management, Rules and Enforcement

The other bank is still too far away to jump or swim to, so you can go no further. You may have improved upon your Current Performance simply by paying strict attention to compliance, management, rules, and enforcement, especially if your organization was careless to begin with. But your Bridge can't carry you all the way to Sustainable Excellence: it's too short and, with just one pillar and no attachment at the other bank, it's wobbly. The first rush of flood waters will weaken and maybe knock it over, as will a hurricane or an earthquake. And you can be sure that your organization will face floods, hurricanes, and earthquakes in the form of changes in the economy, technological advances, aggressive competitors, regulatory changes, pandemics, changes in social norms and customer tastes, and more.

Many organizations have built this first part of the Bridge to Excellence, then stopped. They shuttle back and forth between the bank of Current Performance and the abrupt end of their half-built bridge, frantically trying to deal with problems, doing well one year and backsliding the next. Although they might remain in business for years, they're never the leader, never out in front in sales, innovation, customer service, community relations, employee retention, or anything else. They're never able to push ahead to excellence, and certainly not to Sustainable Excellence. Instead, they devote all their efforts to staying alive.

All they can do is to try to manage the failure rate. That is, a good year will be one with fewer failures. Excellence is simply not part of the conversation. That's because to achieve excellence you need to get to the other shore, and for that you need a full Bridge.

How is the Bridge extended? You begin by building a second pillar, the Culture Pillar, which represents the shared characteristics and beliefs that govern behavior within an organization. Culture is not just what is shared among a group; it is the *why* for what is common. In other words, culture isn't just "the way we do things around here." It's the *why* behind the *way*.

Organizational culture is a teacher, rapidly "instructing" new hires and contractors on how they are to behave. Culture is also an enforcer, often more powerful than the Enforcement Strut on the first part of the Bridge. Indeed, if the Culture Pillar and the Enforcement Strut are misaligned, the Bridge will be weakened.

Rising above the Culture Pillar is the Workers Tower. Workers sit atop culture because they *are* the culture, as reflected in their collective values and behaviors, their eagerness and resentment, their strong attention to their work and equally strong ability to slop through that same work, and much more. And as you'll see, everyone in the organization is part of the culture. Even managers and leaders are a part of the culture, often as a subculture. Everyone included in the culture because everyone works to achieve the organization's goals, although they influence the outcomes in different ways.

In some organizations, the Culture Pillar is the part of the Bridge that changes the most. That's because every time a new employee joins the organization or a contractor comes aboard, even if just for a short while, culture changes, even if imperceptibly. Each new person brings a little different set of beliefs, feelings, expertise, challenges, or what-have-you to the organization and has some impact on the Culture Pillar. Culture shifts every time management issues new rules, every time profits or pay rates go up or down, and every time new technology is introduced; every time so many things happen. This means that the Culture Pillar is constantly being chipped away and is constantly in need of maintenance and repair— sometimes a total overhaul. Otherwise, the Culture Pillar may shift, crack, or crumble and the Bridge will collapse.

The Focus and Reinforcement Struts help to keep this from happening by tying the Culture Pillar more strongly to the Bridge. Focus directs everyone's attention to what really matters. This is vital, for every organization wrestles with problems, questions, failures, successes, workloads, internal changes, external challenges, and other issues, often many at once. Without a Focus Strut, people will be running up and down the Bridge, dealing with the problems they see before their eyes—but those may not be the most important issues at the moment. As a result, problems will pile up and the Bridge may collapse. The Focus Strut keeps everyone's attention riveted on what is most important now. The Reinforcement Strut works hand in hand with the Focus Strut, encouraging people to pay attention to what is most important.

The Focus and Reinforcement Struts tie the Culture Pillar more firmly to the bridge, just as the Rules and

Enforcement Struts shore up the Compliance Pillar. But where rules and enforcement are often treated as negative and punitive, focus and reinforcement can and should be positive and rewarding. Rules and enforcement hold people back, often for good reason. But as you'll see, focus and reinforcement help everyone to see the value in what they have been asked to pay attention to. This encourages them to forge ahead with the confidence and commitment that comes from knowing they're contributing to the organization's success.

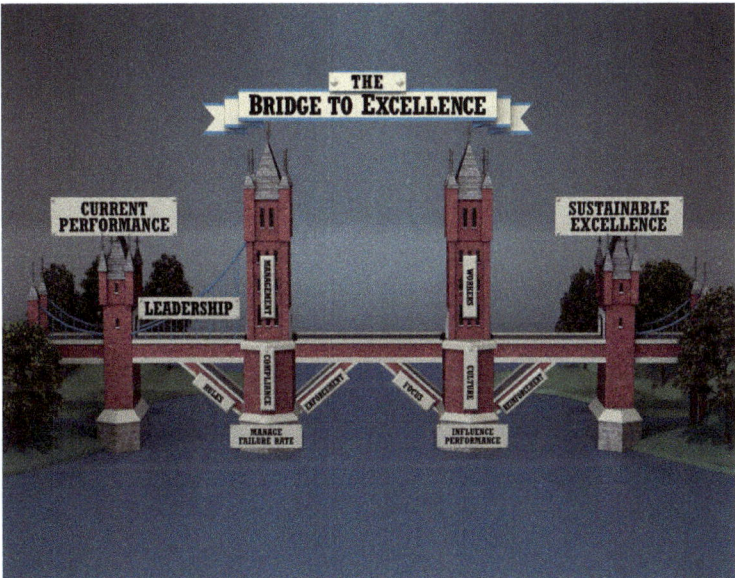

Diagram 4: Workers, Culture, Focus and Reinforcement

The Bridge Gets You There, But . . .

Now, as you can see in diagram 4 your Bridge extends from one bank of the river to the other, from

Current Performance to Sustainable Excellence. But it's a rather basic bridge. There's nothing, for example, to link the Management Tower and Compliance Pillar to the Workers Tower and Culture Pillar. Yes, they're parts of the same bridge, but there's nothing to facilitate communication and cooperation between the two, nothing to stop one from swaying in one direction while the other bends in a different direction. It's as if you have two half-bridges that touch each other but don't function as one.

This will not suffice, so you must connect the two halves at the top of the Bridge with the Leadership Cable, Trust Truss, and Teamwork Cable (See Diagram 5).

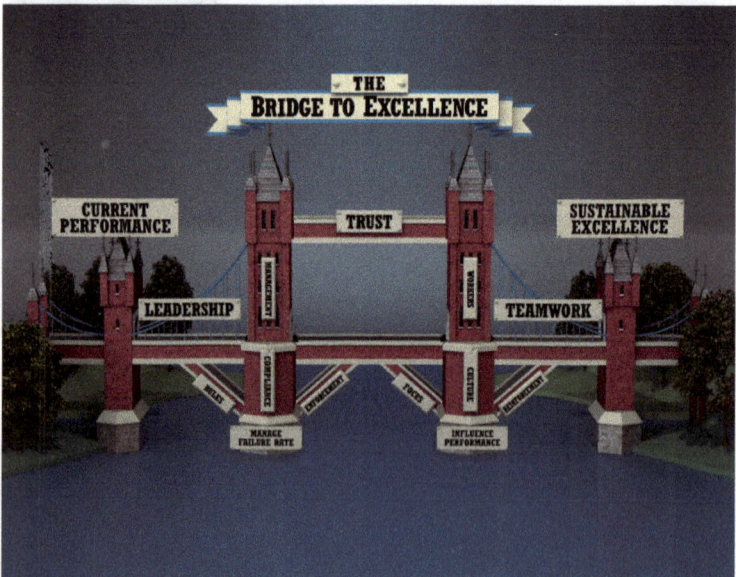

Diagram 5: Leadership, Trust, Teamwork

Leadership is not the same thing as management, which is about making sure the organization is in compliance, that things work, and that work is being done. Leadership is something else entirely. At its best, leadership influences and inspires workers to perform at peak levels, to go above and beyond not because they have to but because they want to. Leadership can then help workers excel by removing obstacles to excellence, obstacles such as silly, time-wasting rules.

The Leadership Cable connects leadership to management, ensuring that leadership and management work in concert. The Trust Truss further firms up the Bridge by linking and ensuring strong communication and cooperation between management and workers. Trust is the glue that holds worker groups and culture together. Early in my corporate career, at FlourDaniel, a team member shared with me that trust means we're all in this together and we're not going to let each other fail.

With the Leadership Cable and Trust Truss in place, with cooperation between management and workers, you can put the Teamwork Cable in place on the far end of the bridge. Ideally, you'll see teamwork between individuals in the same area; between shifts; between departments; between workers, management, and leadership; and between individuals and the organization as a whole.

Your Bridge to Excellence is now complete and robust, carrying you from one bank to the other. Your Bridge will withstand the pressures of water and wind beating against it. Both strong and flexible, it can bear all the usual high waters, storms, earthquakes, and other disturbances it is expected to.

But every once in a while, the unexpected happens. The river's waters rise to frightening levels and flood the banks. Hurricane winds begin to blow, unusually powerful earthquakes rattle your bridge, and rivets begin to pop. The unexpected hits in the form of a pandemic, critical equipment failure, supply chain failure, or inability to secure key components. The unexpected may take a much uglier shape, such as a worksite death or mass casualties— think of the Challenger, Chernobyl, Piper Alpha, Deep Water Horizon, and DuPont La Porte disasters, to name a few. Or perhaps your manufacturing practices lead to deaths outside the workplace. We've seen that happen with the Ford Pinto fuel tank fires and the design flaw with the Boeing 737 Max that led to the crashes of Lion Air Flight 610 and Ethiopian Airlines Flight 302.

It's nearly impossible to plan for the unexpected because, by definition, we don't know what it is, when it will happen, or what form it will take. But while you can't anticipate the unexpected, you can reinforce your Bridge by strengthening your operational capacity to prevent undesirable events as well as your capacity to recover and restore the organization when the unexpected occurs. You do this by beefing up your System Capacity to Prevent and your System Capacity to Recover (see Diagram 6). We all experienced these two systems during the COVID-19 pandemic. Vaccinations, masks, and other preventive measures represented our System Capacity to Prevent becoming ill. Monoclonal antibodies and other anti-viral medications were our System Capacity to Recover in case we became sick.

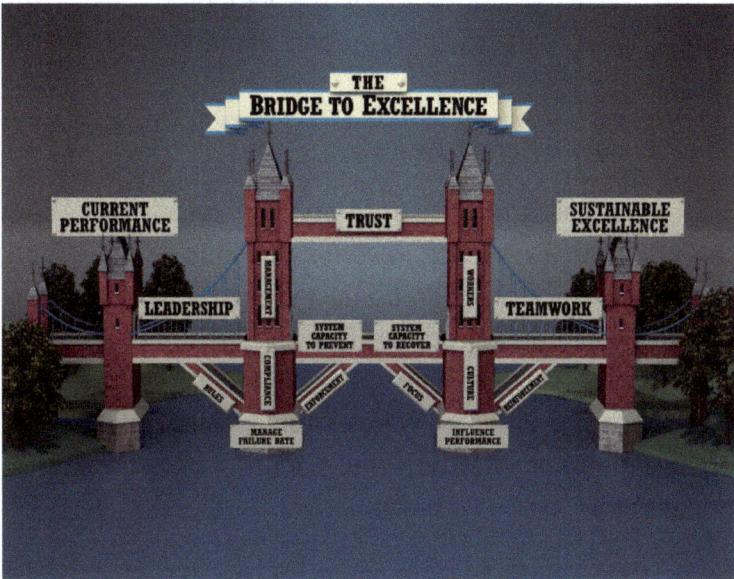

Diagram 6: System Capacity to Prevent and Recover

With the System Capacities to Prevent and Recover in place, you have a complete, robust, and strong yet flexible Bridge to Sustainable Excellence. When the unexpected happens, your Bridge can absorb the shock and you can continue producing excellent results—results of all kinds, including sales, employee retention, teamwork, innovation, or any other metric you might measure. Now you are poised to be the leader in your industry. You are the organization people want to work with and for, to purchase from, and to praise to others.

And you will continue being so, as long as you pay strict attention to the care and maintenance of your Bridge. We'll talk more about the various pieces of the bridges and plus their care and maintenance in the chapters to come.

Same Bridge, Different Views

My background is in safety, so I usually talk about the Bridge to Excellence in terms of reducing risk, safety excellence through operational excellence, and creating highly reliable organizations. This has led some people to think that the Bridge is just about excellence in safety, or that there are different bridges for different parts of an organization, or maybe even bridges upon bridges or bridges in bridges.

No, there's just one Bridge to Sustainable Excellence for the entire organization. Compliance is compliance across the entire organization, leadership is leadership, teamwork is teamwork, and so on. But while it's the same bridge, each area or part of the organization sees the various components through its own lens. Thus, when the safety department looks at the Compliance Pillar, it thinks "OSHA." But when the finance department sees the Compliance Pillar, it thinks "Sarbanes-Oxley," among other things. And when the sales department sees the same pillar, it thinks, among other things, about the Foreign Corrupt Practices Act and not conducting business with countries currently being sanctioned or boycotted by the government.

Although it's the exact same Bridge, each part of the organization has its own way of introducing its people to the Bridge's elements. Thus, when the production department introduces new hires to the Teamwork Cable, it talks about teamwork in terms of helping people lift heavy items, holding ladders steady for fellow workers, and so on. The finance department, on the other hand, talks about teamwork in terms of good emotional intelligence, role and goal clarity, and collaboration.

Even though each department talks about teamwork in different ways, it remains teamwork. Think of it as "same concept, different lens."

We can see examples of "same concept, different lens" in various aspects of life. For example, in the British Military Forces, members of the Army and Air Force salute with the palm of the right hand facing forward as it touches the forehead, while members of the Navy salute with the palm facing down. It's the same "pillar," the same respect for rank, but rendered a little bit differently in different departments of the British Armed Forces.

We can see "same concept, different lens" in sports celebrations. In track, the winning runner might celebrate by taking a lap. In football, the scoring player might slam the ball into the ground. In baseball, players might share high-fives. And in soccer, they might do a group hug. It's the same "Celebration Pillar," with different lenses in different sports.

The same holds true with the Bridge to Excellence. Each department, team, shift, or group within an organization may have a different lens with which to talk about different parts of the Bridge, but it is the same Bridge, the same Compliance, the same Trust, and so on. The Bridge has only one route and one destination: Sustainable Excellence.

Building the Bridge to Excellence Everywhere

The Bridge isn't just for businesses, chambers of commerce, and the like. It's for every organization that wants to develop and sustain excellence.

Think of a large military force such as the US Army. Its Bridge has a very strong Compliance Pillar in the form of regulations and an equally strong Management Tower to make sure everyone is complying and doing the necessary work. New inductees are introduced to the Army's Culture Pillar the moment they step off the bus to begin Basic Training, with endless rules, rituals, and the ever-present drill sergeant to make sure they absorb the culture. And yes, the Army has the Rules, Enforcement, Focus, and Reinforcement struts. All of this makes for a powerful bottom half of the bridge. But even though every single soldier in the Army has been imbued with the elements on the bottom part of the bridge, the whole thing will come crumbling down if the Leadership, Teamwork, and Trust elements are weak. That's because wars are won by regular soldiers going above and beyond, and they will only do so if they are inspired by leadership and have the trust and teamwork necessary for them to excel.

Think of a symphony orchestra. The first half of its bridge is strong indeed, with the conductor serving as management and ensuring compliance: everybody must play the right note at the right time. But lacking the second part of the bridge, the music it creates will be dull. It's only when the orchestra develops a culture of excellence—with the focus on trust and teamwork it takes to get scores of people playing in unison—and when it is led with the inspired leadership that makes music come alive that it will create beauty.

Think of the many scientists across the world who contributed to the creation of the COVID-19 vaccines in a matter of months, not the ten to fifteen years it usually takes. They toiled in a highly pressurized situation, with researchers working in different laboratories at different companies and universities in different countries. Yet they complied with the rules of pharmaceutical development, had incredible focus, had a culture of "we must excel, for lives depend on us," and had the incredible teamwork that allowed them to exchange information with others working at rival labs, companies, and universities. They had all the components of a Bridge to Excellence, and they succeeded.

Think of a sports team, political party, health advocacy group such as the Alzheimer's Association, or any other group with a goal. They all need a strong Bridge to Excellence to be more than simply "in business."

Key Points about the Bridge

- The Bridge to Sustainable Excellence takes you from where you are, Current Performance, to where you want to go, Sustainable Excellence.
- The Bridge carries you over the roiling waters of competition, regulations, pandemics, changing customer tastes, supply chain disruptions, and all the other difficulties you face every day.
- The Bridge is composed of many elements, including the Compliance and Culture Pillars, the Management and Workers Towers, the Leadership and Teamwork Cables, and the Trust Truss.
- Every organization has a Bridge whether they realize it or not, utilize it or not.
- There's just one Bridge for the entire organization, but each area or part of the organization sees the various components through its own lens.
- Sustainable excellence occurs when you create a culture focused on going above and beyond what is necessary to stay in business or collect a paycheck.

Questions to Consider

1. How far has your organization progressed in constructing its Bridge?
2. Which Bridge element, if focused on, would make the biggest difference to your organization in pursuing sustainable excellence?

Chapter Three – *You* are *the Bridge*

When thinking about the Bridge to Excellence, some people imagine a big truck representing their organization driving slowly across, heading toward Sustainable Excellence. Others envision a tow truck pulling a big building across a bridge, with the building representing their organization. Still others think of hundreds of people, representing their organization's leadership, management, and workforce, strolling across.

The Bridge certainly looks like a solid roadway taking you from here to there, just like any physical bridge you go across in everyday life. It seems as if all your organization has to do is start on the Current Performance side and make its way across to Sustainable Excellence. It may take some time to get there, and you may have to stop to handle problems or even back up once in a while. But once you've arrived at the other end, you're all set. Unfortunately, that's not the case. It's not a one-and-done, we-build-it-and-they'll-use-it situation.

That's because there's a major difference between physical bridges like the Golden Gate Bridge and the metaphorical Bridge to Excellence. With physical bridges, there is a clear-cut separation between the bridge's builders and its users. The builders erect the structure and then leave, turning the bridge over to the users. Time passes on and the builders may be long gone or long dead, while the users, who never even think about the builders, continue to traverse the unchanging bridge.

But in the case of our Bridge to Excellence, there is no separation between builders and users. They are one and the same. One set of leaders, managers, and workers does not build the bridge, then turn it over to another set of leaders, managers, and workers to use. This cannot happen, because the Bridge to Excellence cannot be built in the absence of the people who are going to use it, and the Bridge is never finished. Even when the entire structure is in place, when everyone stands back to admire and applaud it, it's not finished. It's constantly being dented and chipped, stressed and cracked, and shaken and broken apart by its users. (And that's not counting the damage caused by outside forces!) It is also constantly being maintained, repaired, and extended by the very same users. Even in the case of long-lived organizations such as Brooks Brothers, which was founded in 1818, the Bridge continues to be both damaged and repaired, trampled upon and built by its users—that is, by the organization itself.

This is a key point: The Bridge to Excellence is not just a means of getting your organization from the beginning to the end of a particular journey. It *is* the organization. It is simultaneously the path to improvement, the people taking that path, and the people maintaining and building the path. And I say "building" the path rather than "rebuilding" to emphasize that every organization's Bridge should change significantly over time. It *must* change; it *must* be periodically redesigned, if for no other reason than that the erosion of time constantly pushes back the destination, Sustainable Excellence, and the bridge must be extended accordingly.

Think about an organization such as Ford Motors, which in 1913 introduced the mass production of cars. What did the fact that the organization was based around assembly-line production mean for its Bridge, assuming they thought in such terms in the early nineteen hundreds? Back then, blue-collar workers were not asked to think much; they simply had to perform a particular motion over and over. Very little collaboration between management and workers was needed. Relatively little trust between workers and leadership was required, for workers did what the bosses told them to do or they were fired. OSHA had not yet been created, and Sarbanes-Oxley and many other regulations had not yet been passed, so compliance with governmental rules and regulations wasn't as pressing an issue as it is today.

For the Ford Motors of 1913, the Bridge was primarily the first half, with management and compliance, rules and enforcement. However, in the one hundred plus years that have passed since the first car rolled off their assembly line, the company's Bridge has grown much stronger and longer and has become more tightly interwoven.

The first part of the Bridge would have to have grown stronger, otherwise Ford Motors would not be able to remain open in an era of greatly increased regulation, with the additional complications created by organized labor, international competition, foreign manufacture, and supply chain issues. And at some point, Ford Motors had to dramatically beef up the second half of its Bridge, for in today's high-tech, highly competitive business environment, leadership desperately wants workers to think, take the initiative, provide input, stop the job when things don't go as planned, and take ownership. All this requires a strong culture, firm leadership, lots of trust, and more—in other words, it requires a robust, fully-formed Bridge.

The ways in which Ford Motors has reshaped its Bridge even while being guided by it are not unique. No organization can stop time, which means every Bridge must evolve and grow with the times.

Remember, the Bridge to Excellence is at the same time the ever-evolving path, the people on the path, and the people maintaining and building the path. This means that every change within the organization, no matter how small, whether brought about internally or externally, causes some change to the Bridge.

There are periodic and obvious changes which occur when, for example, leadership introduces a new strategy or there is a significant layoff. There are regular and predictable changes, like what happens to one of my clients, a project-based oil pipeline construction company with an annual employee turnover rate of eighty percent. Then there are the subtle changes that cannot help but happen in daily operations, even when things are going well. In fact, good times can be dangerous times, for when things are going well people can become complacent and fail to keep the Bridge in good repair.

But continual repair is essential, for every organization's Bridge is constantly being stressed, shaken, tilted, and otherwise altered by the actions, ideas, perceptions, feelings, and even personal events that impact the people in the organization. And many times, it's the quieter, less obvious changes that cause the more serious damage over time. The slight and slow, imperceptible drift of attitudes within a company can cause cracks to appear everywhere. It doesn't take a tsunami to topple a bridge: the drip, drip, drip of worker dissatisfaction, tiny trust erosions, slight failures of focus, or anything else occurring within the organization can, over time, shake your Bridge so severely that you must halt your journey across or even go back to the beginning and start all over again.

Even if your organization only does one thing, over and over, it will be affected by what happens within and by what happens in the larger world.

Think of the Atlanta Braves, which is considered by many to be the oldest continuously operating baseball team in America. You can trace the team all the way back to 1871, although they were called the Red Stockings back then and played in Boston, not Atlanta. From Boston they moved to Milwaukee and finally wound up in Atlanta. During their 150 years or so of existence, they have gone by several names, including the Red Stockings, Beaneaters, Doves, Rustlers, and Braves. The team has been based in three different states, played in eight different home stadiums, been directed by over twenty owners, been led by forty-five different managers, and had a total of nearly two thousand players on their roster. They've been on top, winning six of the first eight pennants in baseball history, and they've gone through lengthy periods of struggle.

Those are just some of the changes that have occurred within the Brave's organization, which are regular and expected in the game of baseball. Many of the changes in the industry and larger world were not anticipated. Since their founding, the Braves have weathered two world-wide pandemics and two world wars, survived tremendous contractions and expansions in the national economy, seen rival teams rise and fall, gone from being representatives of the national pastime to the third-choice national sport (behind football and basketball), and traversed baseball's dead-ball, live-ball, integration, expansion, free agency, long-ball and steroid eras. Whatever Bridge to Excellence they used in 1871,

1907, 1933, 1945, 1993, or 2001—assuming they had bridges—would simply not do the job today.

No Bridge to Excellence can be fixed and unchanging, not if you want to achieve lasting excellence. It *will* change as the organization changes, and it *must* change in response to outside conditions.

The key thing to remember is that the Bridge to Excellence is not just a transportation mode. It is simultaneously you *and* your path *and* your never-ending project.

Now let's take a look at the various elements of the Bridge and see how they, collectively, carry you to Sustained Excellence.

Key Points about You and Your Organization's Bridge

- Your Bridge to Excellence is not just a transportation mode. It is simultaneously you, your path, and your never-ending project.
- The Bridge is not just a means of getting your organization from the beginning to the end of a particular journey. Your Bridge *is* your organization.
- Building the Bridge is not a one-and-done, we-build-it-and-they'll-use-it situation.
- Every organization's Bridge should change significantly over time, if for no other reason than that the erosion of time constantly pushes back the destination, Sustainable Excellence, and your Bridge must be extended accordingly.
- Continual maintenance and repair are essential, for every organization's Bridge is constantly being

stressed, shaken, tilted, and otherwise altered by the actions, ideas, perceptions, feelings, and even personal events that impact the people in the organization.

Questions to Consider

1. What are your most important responsibilities with respect to building the Bridge for your organization?

2. What are your most important responsibilities with respect to ensuring proactive maintenance on your organization's Bridge?

Chapter Four – Management and Compliance

In 2009, financier Bernie Madoff pled guilty to charges that he had been running a multi-decade, multi-billion-dollar fraud. The essence of his scheme was simple: promise people large returns if they invest with you, take their money but don't invest it, send your investors phony statements showing great returns, sit back as the people brag about their earnings to others, take money from a new batch of people eager to earn large returns, and repeat.

This is a Ponzi Scheme, named for Charles Ponzi, an Italian immigrant who, in 1919, opened a company in Boston which would sell business ideas to Europe. It was in this office that Ponzi received an international reply coupon, which can be redeemed for a certain amount of international postage in the recipient's country. A business in France, for example, might purchase the international reply coupon in Paris, put it in the envelope along with their letter, and send it to a contact in Boston. That person would use the coupon to buy American stamps to reply to the business in France. It was a way of giving your correspondent postage for the return letter without you having to buy stamps in the other country.

Ponzi quickly realized that, due to inflation and currency fluctuations, there was a difference between the costs and values of these coupons in different countries. This meant, for example, you might be able to buy a coupon in France for the equivalent of $1, exchange it in America for stamps worth $1.20, sell the $1.20 worth of stamps and pocket the difference. This is simple arbitrage, but in Ponzi's hands it became much more.

Ponzi created the Securities Exchange Company, claiming he would make incredible profits by buying the coupons in one country, selling them in others, and returning a big slice of the difference to his clients as profit. People invested quite a bit of money with him, and in less than a year Ponzi was raking in the bucks, taking a generous portion of the returns for his efforts. He lived in a mansion, purchased the must-have car of the day (called the Locomobile), and made investments in other companies. He even won a libel lawsuit when a financial writer pointed out that it was impossible for Ponzi to be making such incredible returns in so little time. But the writer was right: Ponzi's program was a fraud based on fooling people into giving him money for investments he wasn't actually making.

Ponzi's scheme crashed and he was sentenced to five years in prison on federal charges—he later served more time on state charges. It is estimated that his investors lost $20 million, which would be about $200 million in 2022 dollars. Bernie Madoff's version of Ponzi's scheme cost his investors about $18 billion.

Madoff, Ponzi, and the many others who ran similar schemes didn't concern themselves with compliance, with following the applicable rules and regulations. Rules and regulations vary from industry to industry, country to country, and change through the years. But there is always some version of compliance, some things you must do else you be penalized by the government, your customers, or other parties. Even in ancient Babylonia, back in 1700 BC, you had to follow the business rules inscribed in the Code of Hammurabi. For example, Law 261 says, "If any one hire a herdsman for cattle or sheep, he shall pay him eight gur of corn per annum." And Law 229 says, "If a builder builds a house for some one, and does not construct it properly, and the house which he built fall in and kill its owner, then that builder shall be put to death."[2]

Today, failure to comply can lead to serious consequences, including death of the organization. It is management's first job to make sure the organization and everyone in it is in compliance.

Layers on Layers

The Bridge to Excellence rests on two pillars rising up from the waters. The first of these is the Compliance Pillar, which represents the efforts the organization makes to follow all the necessary federal, state, local, industry, internal, and perhaps international laws, rules, regulations, and guidelines, as well as contractual obligations and the expectations of customers, partners, and others.

As you look at the Compliance Pillar, you can't help but notice that it seems to flow right into the Management Tower above, as if they were a single, rigid, monolith, demanding that everyone obey, comply, conform! But the reality is much more complex than that. Yes, compliance is

---

[2] L. W. King, trans., *The Code of Hammurabi*, Yale Law School, Lillian Goldman Law Library, Avalon Project, https://avalon.law.yale.edu/ancient/hamframe.asp.

a key issue and management is heavily focused on getting people to do what they are supposed to do. In a sense, compliance is management and management is compliance; one is the action, the other the actor. But there are several layers to compliance which, when stacked atop each other, carry management from narrowly focused enforcement up to encouragement to excel.

Imagine, for the sake of this discussion, that the Management-Compliance pillar is made up of numerous layers, like books stacked one atop the other. Management's very first job—the bottom-most layer—is to make it possible for the organization to operate. This means ensuring that it complies with all the laws, rules, and regulations regarding employment, insurance, licenses, taxes, and much more. If the organization is operating in other countries in addition to the United States, management must ensure compliance with additional sets of laws, rules, and regulations. Depending on what product or service they offer, they may also have to make sure that certain employees follow governmental regulations regarding licensure and other matters.

All of this bottom-layer compliance is necessary just to keep the organization's doors open. If management fails in this basic responsibility, the enterprise will be hit with governmental notices, fines, and lawsuits. Word of this will spread, and some customers, banks, suppliers, and partners will decline to work with the business, which will eventually either fail or be shut down by the government.

Above this very basic layer in the Management-Compliance pillar is the layer representing industry standards and requirements, such as medical board certification for physicians or National Dance Teachers Association certification for teachers of ballroom dance. These are often necessary, though not legally required. A state medical license, for example, gives one legal permission to function as a physician, but board certification in anesthesiology, cardiology, or some other specialty may be required for doctors to secure hospital privileges, attract patients, and get the necessary insurance. Certifications and the like may not be legally mandatory, but failure to get them can doom a business to second-class status or worse. Several years ago, the University Medical Center of El Paso, Texas, was hit with a preliminary denial of their accreditation because employees in the center's sterilization unit did not have the proper certifications.[3] Without certification, the hospital could not be accredited. Lacking that accreditation, the hospital could not receive payments from private insurers and government sources and would probably have to close.

Yet another layer in the Management-Compliance pillar represents the internal rules and regulations that management must enforce. These include dictates that come from leadership, as well as rules generated by departments within the organization or by outside

---

[3] Aileen B. Flores, "El Paso's University Medical Center Faces Preliminary Denial of Accreditation," *El Paso Times*, July 10, 2015, https://www.elpasotimes.com/story/archives/2015/07/10/el-pasos-university-medical-center-faces-preliminary-denial/73899738/.

advisers, experts, and consultants. Failure to comply with these rules will not put the organization at odds with the law but may cause trouble within the company. For example, if headquarters decrees that bathroom breaks must be limited to exactly eight minutes, as happened in a Norwegian call center,[4] and one shift or unit enforces that rule while another does not, some employees are going to be doubly unhappy: first, for having to hurry, and second, for feeling like someone else is getting a special favor while they are not.

Another layer represents complying with customer or client contracts and expectations. This can be a major issue, particularly for a company that uses contractors and subcontractors to perform the actual work, and which deals with clients having different requirements regarding environmental protection standards, diversity and inclusion, or other issues. A single subcontractor might have to adhere to several different sets of rules, depending on which of the company's clients it is working for. And the company has to make sure the rules are being followed, even though they vary from customer to customer or site to site.

Sometimes, non-compliance gets you a warning notice. Other times, the cost of not complying is quite substantial. For example, take the following:

---

[4] Emily DiNuzzo, "12 Ridiculous Office Rules That Companies Have Enforced," *Readers Digest*, updated June 16, 2022, https://www.rd.com/list/ridiculous-office-rules-that-companies-enforced/.

- Credit Suisse "was found guilty of conspiring to help Americans evade taxes, resulting in a fine of $2.5 billion."[5]
- Braskem CEO Jose Carlos Grubisich was given a twenty-month jail sentence "for his role in a scheme to divert hundreds of millions of dollars in bribe payments from Braskem to government officials and political parties in Brazil."[6]
- In 2014, Anadarko Petroleum "paid $5.15 billion in a settlement against environmental contamination."[7]
- In 2013, a Safety Manager for the Shaw Group was sentenced to six-and-a-half years in prison for lying about worker injuries and falsifying injury records so his company could collect government bonuses for safety.[8]
- In 2012, GlaxoSmithKline "pleaded guilty for promoting drugs for unapproved uses, kickbacks to physicians and failure in reporting breaches in safety data, resulting in the biggest healthcare fraud in the history of the US, and a $3 billion fine,

---

[5] Ty Haqqi, "15 Biggest Corporate Fines in History." *Yahoo Finance*, February 3, 2021, https://finance.yahoo.com/news/15-biggest-corporate-fines-history-161224674.html.

[6] Kyle Brasseur, "Es-Braskem CEO Gets 20 Months in Jail for Bribery Scheme," *Compliance Week*, October 12, 2021, https://www.complianceweek.com/regulatory-enforcement/ex-braskem-ceo-gets-20-months-in-prison-over-bribery-scheme/30925.article.

[7] Ty Haqqi, "15 Biggest Corporate Fines in History."

[8] Jeff Derango, "Safety Manager Receives Jail Sentence for Falsifying Records," *OSHA.net*, May 22, 2013, https://www.osha.net/osha-news/safety-manager-receives-jail-sentence-for-falsifying-records/.

which is still the largest settlement by a pharmaceutical company."[9]

- Bank and financial services institution HSBC was forced to fork over "$1.256 billion to the US Department of Justice for its role in the violation of US sanctions and anti-money laundering regulations."[10]

Moving Up from Negative to Positive Compliance

So far these compliance matters—these layers—in the lower portion of the Management-Compliance pillar are must-do issues. If management can't handle these tasks, the organization will suffer governmental wrath and public disdain; there will be dissention in the ranks and angry customers or clients demanding fixes or refunds.

In a sense, these are all negative compliance issues, concerned with preventing bad things from happening. But in organizations wishing to excel, management must go beyond avoiding the bad. It must also identify and encourage the good things that need to happen for it to achieve excellence.

Instead of just saying, "This is what we must do to stay alive," it can add, "And if we do these additional things, we will thrive." In practical terms, this means going from "Who is to blame?" to "What system failed or what influenced this?" It means going from "We need to retrain" to "Let's address what led to the decision or deviation from expected outcomes." It means going from

---

[9] Ty Haqqi, "15 Biggest Corporate Fines in History."
[10] Ty Haqqi, "15 Biggest Corporate Fines in History."

making an effort to fail less to pursuing success or excellence. To accomplish this shift in mindset, the organization must think carefully about what management is and what it should strive for.

On the typical organizational chart, management sits between workers and senior leaders, its job being to get the workers below to do what bosses above desire. The three levels have totally different jobs: leadership sets direction, management executes and ensures adherence to direction, and workers comply. Standard definitions support this idea by making sharp distinctions between management and leadership and assigning them totally different sets of duties. For example, management is concerned with ensuring goals are met, failures are reduced, and customers (internal and external) are happy, while senior leadership deals with establishing vision, mission, values, and the strategic framework.

But on the Bridge to Excellence, management is not totally separate from leadership. As the Management-Compliance pillar works its way through the layers of compliance, beginning at strict regulatory compliance and moving up, it meets the Leadership Cable near the top of the bridge. This is because when management functions at its higher levels, it moves from just managing hands and feet to moving hearts and minds, from managing processes and outcomes to managing people. At this point, management becomes more and more like leadership, eventually uniting with leadership at the top of the Bridge. There, management takes on a key function of leadership, which is to inspire others to follow and to contribute to the pursuit of the organization's vision. Compliance gives way to encouragement. Rather than just holding everyone's feet to the fire, management inspires everyone to voluntarily go beyond. In a sense, management and leadership merge at this high level, collectively encouraging everyone in the organization to work toward the greater goal for the benefit of the customers or clients, of the organization, and of each and every member of the organization.

Leadership certainly wants compliance with all laws, rules, regulations, and guidelines; it wants management and workers to keep the organization chugging along. But that will only take a business so far, to an average level at best. Companies wishing to excel have to go beyond negative must-do compliance and start reaching for want-to-do compliance; they must inspire an organization-wide embrace of leadership's vision of excellence. This is the positive compliance that excellent organizations strive for.

Many Ways to Embrace the Good

There are numerous layers to the Management-Compliance pillar and numerous ways management can go beyond negative compliance to embrace the positive. One of the key steps is helping everyone to know, understand, and embrace the organization's vision and values. Most everyone will work for a paycheck, some diligently so. But to become excellent, the organization must be filled with and propelled by people eager to go beyond average.

Think of how Mahatma Gandhi's vision of a free India was embraced by millions of people who risked jail and worse in pursuit of that vision. And it wasn't just anger over British taxes that convinced so many American colonists to take up arms against their king, risking it all in a war against the mighty English army and navy. It was values like those trumpeted by Patrick Henry, who stood up in the Virginia legislature to proclaim, "I know not what course others may take; but as for me, give me liberty or give me death!"

It was visions like those of Martin Luther King, Jr., whose stirring words, "I have a dream," inspired millions to battle for civil rights. It was visions like those of Winston Churchill who, in the darkest days of World War II, stood up in the House of Commons and said, "Let us therefore brace ourselves to our duties, and so bear ourselves that, if the British Empire and its Commonwealth last for a thousand years, men will still say, 'This was their finest hour.'"

Don't get me wrong: every organization absolutely needs compliance, even of the most negative sort. In some industries, certain things absolutely must be enforced and very rigidly so. For example, in food manufacturing, commercial air travel, nuclear research, and power generation, even the slightest deviations can lead to disaster, so the rules must be strictly enforced.

In organizations with hefty turnover, management has no choice but to focus heavily on training and compliance with laws, rules, and regulations and on building controls to prevent humans from making common mistakes.

In low-margin industries—such as fast food, lawn and garden supply stores, auto dealers, furniture stores, and assisted living and retirement homes—management must focus on process, getting the product out or the service completed in the most consistent and economical manner.

Compliance is absolutely necessary and, in some cases, there can be absolutely no deviation from strict adherence. But when building your Bridge, remember that even though the Management Tower sits atop the Compliance Pillar, looking like an enforcer, management should be concerned with more than negative compliance. Management can soar up to merge with leadership at the highest levels of the Bridge. And when leadership and management come together in the genuine desire to inspire the workforce, to spread the organization's vision and values to everyone, management becomes a powerful link between Leadership and Workers and is well trusted by all. With leadership linked to management at the highest levels of the Bridge, with trust running strong between management and workers, your Bridge to Excellence is taking form.

Insights from Industry Leaders

I asked leaders from a number of industries—including for-profit, non-profit, and governmental—for their insights into management and compliance.

With respect to management, I asked: What are some examples of activities or processes leaders must consistently manage within your work or company?

Here are some of their answers:

Kolin Ibrahim, senior manager, environmental, health, and safety, Hess Corporation

- Set annual objectives; set expectations on performance and behaviors.
- Provide materials, tools, and equipment for team members to deliver their work.
- Confirm they are in roles where they have the opportunity to do their best daily.
- Provide recognition and praise for good work to team members every seven days.
- Care about team members as persons; confirm they have friends at work.
- Hold regular one-on-one performance reviews.
- Hold annual development reviews; support team members' learning and growth.

Tobias Read, founder, AQRA Group

- Set a clear cultural direction which is relevant to your business and which sets you up for success. Communicate regularly via different mechanisms. Lead by example. Praise those who exhibit strong cultural alignment and fire those who maintain consistent cultural misalignment.
- Maintain a cadence of regular, uninterrupted, weekly oversight and review to learn from the large and small lessons, and to provide helpful feedback and ensure continual improvement.

- Complete periodic external audits across all areas of business and operations to gain an independent perspective and to spot things that are not visible or otherwise communicated.

Michael J. Devane, vice president of operations, CertainTeed

- Continuous, improvement-focused processes must be created for daily, weekly, monthly, and annual practices to leverage the limited resources businesses have to deliver year-over-year improvements. Leadership discipline, with accurate and timely data, is key to each of these processes' success.

Chris Boleman, president and chief executive officer, Houston Livestock Show and Rodeo

- Follow up after meetings. Meetings happen all the time, but the key is to make sure there is product coming from the meetings and that there is follow-up. One of the most frustrating things for me as a leader is when we have meetings, and in the very next meeting, we are having the exact same discussions. That means we didn't do the work in between the meetings. Therefore, documenting action items and next steps is a *must* and must always be managed.
- You have to have a strategic plan, one with objectives and measures. And employees have to know where their work fits into this strategic plan, to the point of being held accountable for that work. For employees to feel valued, our job is managers is to make sure they know that they and

their work fit within the organizational strategic plan and roadmap.

Jim Cusick, director of manufacturing, Shaw Industries (retired)

- Performance experience (Px): This is our approach for performance management and personal development. We try to co-create with you and your supervisors on task and development goals.
- Manage change.
- Utilize the ADKAR process:
    o Awareness of the need for change
    o Desire to participate and support the change
    o Knowledge on how to change
    o Ability to implement desired skills & behaviors
    o Reinforcement to sustain the change

Jared Matthias, vice president of executive accounts, ChampionX

- Safety programs, processes, trends, key performance indicators (KPIs), incidences (good and bad), safety expectations and performance
- Health of the business through financial metrics, particularly from profit and loss statement and various other financial reporting methods
- Five-year business plans (who, what, when, where, why, which technologies and what are the risks and opportunities)
- Talent management: successions plans, employee training, organizational talent reviews, 9-box grid (a tool used to analyze, display, and compare employee work performance and potential)

- Business plan reviews on performance to plan, as well as marketing and technology reviews and delivering innovation to enable growth to meet the business plan

Mike Diezi, executive director, Spec's Wine, Spirits & Finer Foods

- Communication is critical. No matter what business, project, club, or cause in which one may be involved, the basic tenets of leadership are always the same. Leadership is more of an art than a science; there are so many ways to approach the process properly and so many styles that will prove successful. But no matter which style you, the leader artist, may use, the medium you work in is the same: people. People need to have the opportunity to understand a process or culture if you want to gain their commitment. One cannot motivate people to put their best efforts behind a project, cause, or person without good communication.

Michael Middleton, safety and health director, Georgia Power

- As a leader of an organization, it's imperative that you know the pulse of your culture. Yes, spreadsheets, metrics, and data are all important, and you must inspect what you expect. However, to truly know the pulse of your culture, you have to be willing to engage with front-line employees, work beside them, get to know them and their challenges, and develop processes to enhance their experience in your organization.

Here's an example: When I first received the proverbial "keys to the organization" with my first mid-level leadership role, there was no how-to manual provided. Early in my role, I failed to respect the importance of getting to know the micro-cultures that existed within my organization. That failure in my leadership showed up one day when a distribution lineman in my organization had a serious accident. As my teammate was performing a routine task of lowering a light on a distribution pole, the teammate did not recognize a 14.4kV primary voltage riser on the back of the pole. As the teammate was drilling a hole into the pole, the teammate drilled directly into the primary conductor and a primary flash occurred in his face. Leadership matters. What I later learned was that this teammate had so many personal things going on in his life. The personal things carried over into the work environment and had not been resolved or addressed by local leadership. Since this event, my process for getting to know my teammates and the pulse of my culture is much more engaging. I challenge others to consider the same.

With respect to compliance, I asked, What comes to mind when you think of maintaining compliance as you conduct business? What type of compliance is most important to your ability to operate as a business?

Here are some of their answers:

Mark Kehne, plant manager, Cardinal FG

- Our hierarchy of compliance includes federal and state regulatory compliance, including OSHA, EPA, DNR, and DHS. This is followed by corporate compliance with primarily human resources, benefits, and financial guidelines, and then compliance with local policies, procedures, and protocols. All levels of this hierarchy have an equal influence on our ability to operate as a business. While the formal penalties for non-compliance are potentially more severe for federal and state regulatory controls, the human penalties—such as injuries, impact on compensation, job security, and professional advancement—are more dependent upon compliance with corporate and local controls.

Tobias Read, founder, AQRA Group

- Compliance with regulatory requirements regarding bribery and corruption if dealing overseas, as failure to do so can lead to terminal consequences such as incarceration for the CEO, huge fines and reputational damage that may lead to the collapse of a company
- Compliance with professional rules governing licenses, for failure to do so could lead to the loss of trading licenses
- Compliance with customer contracts, which may be quite unique, for failure to follow can lead to financial penalties, contract cancelation, and in the worst case, legal claims

Michael J. Devane, vice president of operations, CertainTeed

- Respect in the workplace is a fundamental principle that must be clearly communicated and reinforced daily by site leadership. This is the foundation to building trust, which drives collaboration and teamwork, which in turn delivers collective improvement in all functional areas. For instance, in safety, working in a trusting environment encourages employees to share unsafe actions and conditions very readily, knowing leadership will act to improve the process and not blame the people.

Francis Charbonneaux, infrastructure and risk manager, Essity Operations France

> To be in compliance helps us to work with more serenity, but this is not enough to ensure health and safety in daily operations. All types of compliance are important, but for me the first one is to comply with country regulations and all health and safety rules (external and internal).

Chris Boleman, president and chief executive officer, Houston Livestock Show and Rodeo

- Compliance can be defined a number of ways. In leading a non-profit, what first comes to mind is our ability to be proper stewards of our financials. This is critical to our work.
- Most importantly, as the leader, what behaviors do you tolerate? If negativity is around you and there are pockets of people that love to dwell on the negative, as the leader, do you tolerate this behavior? Everyone is watching what you do.

- One thing I do is send a positive note every single Monday. It could be something in the world, something on the team, or a message from me on leadership. My theory is if I do it, positivity becomes just as contagious as negativity.

Jared Matthias, vice president of executive accounts, ChampionX

- Safety compliance, that is, total recordable incident rate (TRIR) and total vehicle accident rate (TVAR) are your ticket to the party. Without a rate that's equal to or better than the set rate for your industry, you won't even get a seat at the table.
- Employee rights and work policies
- Expense compliance
- Bribery, state and or government official(s) awareness in foreign countries
- Financial compliance across international businesses, joint ventures, distributorships, partnerships, and so on. There is an enormous amount of pitfalls in these arrangements.

Ed Senavaitis, director of corporate safety, Buckeye Partners, LP

- Compliance isn't really a measure; it's an expectation. To me, measuring adherence to our visions, mission, and values is most important.

Joel Simon, partner, Fernelius and Simon

- Obviously, compliance with the laws that apply to a business are paramount. A close second is compliance with the culture and "brand" inherent to any business.

Mike Diezi, executive director, Spec's Wine, Spirits & Finer Foods

- The company I work for is large and there are many diverse areas involved. There are also many different sets of rules and regulations based on the products we sell: liquor, cigars, wine, beer, food, and CBD products. When we build new stores, we work with inspectors and fire marshals. We also have almost two hundred locations across the state, along with warehouses, which involves safety and operational protocols. We must first comply with all things from the legal aspect of the heavily regulated industry. Many of these rules and regulations are in place for safety measures. It is beneficial as a company for us to follow these guidelines, even if they were not a formal regulation. For instance, a safety harness and training for a forklift operator is a good practice for a company, even if OSHA did not require it. The logic is simple, because as leaders we always want to protect our most valuable resource, our people.

Najya Al Hinai, continuous improvement lead, MSEML

- The upstream oil and gas industry is faced with multiple risks. Regulatory compliance is key to maintaining the reputation, transparency, growth, security, and value generation of the business. Our risks across the board are monitored and reviewed annually to ensure we work toward decreasing or eliminating risks, appropriately managing and complying with the requests of regulatory bodies.

Commander Richard H. Tetrev, US Navy (retired)

- Compliance is very different in the military compared to the civilian world, and it varies in degrees between peace time and war. In war, when an order is given, there can be no hesitation from those that receive the order. Every individual has an integral part to play, and it takes all working together, doing their part, to be functional. Every member of the group must have rehearsed their part so many times that they know exactly what to do. Then the group will do the same and the group will become one.

Michael Middleton, safety and health director, Georgia Power

- Very early in my career, I was told by a leader, "It's never right to do wrong to do right." When I think about compliance, I think about this statement. Often—be it financial, safety, data entry, and so on—your teammates, in the spirit of attempting to do what they think is the right thing, can end up making a mess and violating your rules and regulations.

Key Points about Management and Compliance

- Failure to comply to an often bewildering number and variety of rules, regulations, and expectations can lead to serious consequences, including the death of the organization.
- It is management's first job to make sure the organization and everyone in it is in compliance.

- Compliance is management and management is compliance; one is the action, the other the actor.
- In organizations wishing to excel, management must go beyond avoiding the bad. It must also identify and encourage the good things that need to happen for it to achieve excellence.
- To become excellent, the organization must be filled with and propelled by people eager to go beyond average.

Questions to Consider

1. On a scale of one to ten, with one indicating you have yet to begin and ten that you are there, how would you rate the effectiveness and completeness of the compliance element of your organization's Bridge?
2. What, if improved, would add value to your efforts to ensure compliance?
3. On the same scale of one to ten, what score would you give for the effectiveness of the management element of your organization's Bridge?
4. What are management's most important responsibilities in terms of building and maintaining your organization's Bridge?

Chapter Five – Rules and Enforcement

Since the late 1970s, when American businesses began outsourcing production to developing countries, forced labor has become a major concern. Western companies have been accused of ignoring the fact that factory workers have been made to toil for long stretches without a day off and work up to sixteen hours per day and that children have been forced to work in mines under terrible conditions, digging by hand the mineral ores necessary to produce high-tech devices.

In 2019, Judge Carl Nichols of the Unites States District Court for the District of Columbia was assigned to oversee a lawsuit that accused Apple, Microsoft, and other tech companies of, in effect, condoning forced labor and child trafficking when they agreed to work with certain overseas firms. The case was filed on behalf of children who had been hurt or killed while working in cobalt mines in the Democratic Republic of Congo. In 2021, Judge Nichols dismissed the case, ruling that "the plaintiffs had failed to establish a connection between the cobalt mines where the children were injured and their causal relationship to the tech companies."[11]

Perhaps Judge Nichols was right on the law, perhaps not, but he has since been accused of breaking the rules—specifically, of violating Section 455 of the US

---

[11] David Jeans, "A Federal Judge Bought Apple and Microsoft Bonds while Overseeing a Case against Them — Then Dismissed It," *Forbes*, June 24, 2022, https://www.forbes.com/sites/davidjeans/2022/06/24/federal-judge-apple-microsoft-conflict-of-interest/.

Code, which instructs judges to recuse themselves if their impartiality can be challenged. It's important to note that Section 455 doesn't say a judge must recuse himself if he actually favors one side or the other, simply if his "impartiality might reasonably be questioned."

The relevant portion of Section 455 says that judges, justices, or magistrates should recuse themselves if "he knows that he, individually or as a fiduciary, or his spouse or minor child residing in his household, has a financial interest in the subject matter in controversy or in a party to the proceeding"[12]

While Judge Nichols was presiding over the case, he purchased bonds issued by Apple on seven different occasions and bought Microsoft bonds five times. When he was accused of being partial to Apple and Microsoft because he had a financial interest in those companies, Nichols claimed that because he bought company bonds, not stocks, he did not have a financial interest in the companies. Therefore, he was not partial to Apple or Microsoft and did not violate Section 455. Legal scholars disagree, and the plaintiffs in the case, the ones representing the children and their families, are appealing the judge's decision.

Judge Nichols is not alone in appearing to break Section 455. In 2021, the *Wall Street Journal* published the results of their investigation which revealed that, over the past decade, 131 federal judges involved in 685 court

---

[12] "28 U.S. Code § 455 - Disqualification of justice, judge, or magistrate judge," Cornell Law School Legal Information Institute, https://www.law.cornell.edu/uscode/text/28/455.

cases could be accused of partiality to a party in a case they were handling because either they or their family members owned stock in companies involved. And about two-thirds of the 131 judges ruled in such a way that their personal financial interests benefited.[13]

Section 455 seems to be clearly stated, but like all rules, it can be reinterpreted, stretched, broken, or disregarded by workers, unknowingly or deliberately.

The Well-Made Rules Strut

Like judges, organizations must follow certain rules. The must obey the laws, rules, and regulations issued by federal, state, local, and possibly foreign governments. They may have to comply with industry guidelines, contractual restrictions, and the unwritten "laws" representing the expectations of their clients, customers, suppliers, and partners. They may also have to bend to social pressures which may demand, for example, that they be "green" or support certain states' laws regarding abortion and other sensitive issues.

Falling out of compliance with the laws, rules, regulations, guidelines, expectations, and demands of multiple government entities, clients, customers, suppliers, partners, financial backers, and/or society in general can lead to legal problems, financial stress,

---

[13] Debra Cassens Weiss, "131 Federal Judges Oversaw Cases Involving Companies in Which They or Their Families Owned Stock," *ABA Journal*, September 29, 2021, https://www.abajournal.com/news/article/131-federal-judges-oversaw-cases-involving-companies-in-which-they-or-their-families-owned-stock.

shutdowns, reputational damage, boycotts, and bankruptcy. Compliance with all the necessary rules is essential, which is why the Bridge to Excellence firmly anchors the Compliance Pillar to the Bridge with a Rules Strut.

An organization with a well-made Rules Strut will:

- assemble all the laws, rules, regulations, guidelines, contractual requirements, expectations and demands relevant to the organization,
- organize and present them in an understandable manner, and
- teach the pertinent ones to members of the organization, depending on their duties and needs.

Ideally, the Rules Strut organizes, presents, and teaches the rules in such a way that makes compliance understandable, agreeable, and easy and in so doing enhances production, customer service, and everything else the organization does.

In a sense, the Rules Strut is a combination filter and magnifier, eliminating the confusion that arises when too many rules are dumped on workers and making it easier for everyone to see and understand exactly what they need to know. Unfortunately, some organizations fall short when setting up their Rules Strut, falling into the traps of accountabilism, dipping the herd, not spreading the news, implementing too many rules, letting rules conflict with requirements, and neglecting the *why*. Let's look at these strut-sappers.

Strut-Sapper #1 – Accountabilism

"As Haiti goes hungry, tons of food rot at ports." So reads the headline of a 2008 NBC News story, which explains that Haitian officials, concerned about the large amount of drug smuggling conducted at their ports, instituted a series of strict rules designed to put an end to smuggling, once and for all. Unfortunately, the rules tied the ports up in endless red tape, and endless amounts of donated food—beans, rice, and more—sat in the sun at the ports so long that it rotted. Starving in the midst of plenty, desperate Haitians mixed salt, vegetable oil, and dirt together to make "cookies" to fill their bellies.[14]

More recently, a company I worked with grew alarmed at the number of incidents involving their company-owned trucks. So, they instituted a 360-degree walk-around policy which required drivers to walk all the way around their trucks before starting them up, checking for obstacles, little animals or children in the wheel wells, and other problems. This is not unusual in the industry, for nobody wants to see a vehicle cause damage to property or person. But then, in response to a few more incidents, this company went further and instituted a new policy: every time a driver wants to back up, no matter what the situation or distance, he has to call a supervisor for permission—every single time, even after doing the walk around.

---

[14] Associated Press, "As Haiti Goes Hungry, Tons of Food Rot at Ports," *NBC News*, March 6, 2008, https://www.nbcnews.com/id/wbna23507559.

These are examples of what David Weinberger calls "accountabilism," trying to account for every little aspect of compliance with a rule—or five, ten, or fifty rules. Organizations do this even when some of the rules don't make a lot of sense, get in the way of work, or contradict each other.

Not only that, accountabilism turns supervisors into paper pushers. More policies and more procedures inevitably mean more paperwork and more meetings—and more phone calls to approve things like backing trucks up. This has a downstream effect on supervisors who would like to be with the workers, giving feedback, coaching, and removing obstacles and barriers, instead of being stuck in their offices filling out forms. But when these supervisors are told they aren't doing enough supervising, they say, "Tell me what form I can *stop* filling out, tell me what meeting you *don't* want me to go to."

Your organization is accountabilist if, when something unwanted happens, rather than trying to figure out why the problem occurred and dealing with it at the source, you pass new rules. Over time, rules pile upon rules, and soon it's impossible to organize, present, and teach a simple set of understandable rules that helps people accomplish their tasks.

Accountabilism is to rules what barnacles are to boats: ugly, unwanted clumps that create drag and force everyone to work harder to keep moving ahead. Accountabilist rules need to be scraped away often and with vigor.

Strut-Sapper #2 – Dipping the Herd

A related approach is called "dipping the herd." This phrase comes from animal husbandry and describes what happens when some cattle in a herd are infested with ticks. The rancher can't know how many others are infested, so the entire herd is "dipped" by being made to walk through a vat of liquid medicine that comes up to their heads.

Suppose someone in your finance department deliberately skipped a couple of steps, and now your company is out of compliance with Sarbanes-Oxley. The offender knew exactly what they were supposed to do but intentionally broke the rules. Leadership knows exactly who's at fault and why, but instead of holding the offender accountable, they decide to "dip the herd" by issuing a new, larger, set of rules for the Finance Department. From now on, instead of having to work through, say, five steps to accomplish a certain task and remain in compliance with Sarbanes-Oxley, everyone will have to go through ten steps. Is it any surprise that members of the Finance Department will be angry at management? That they will think something like, "That bozo intentionally bypassed steps, and your response is to make *me* take more steps? What's going to prevent the same bozo from breaking these rules, too? Or the next bozo?"

The federal government recently dipped the entire US population by issuing new regulations requiring PayPal and other payment platforms to report to the IRS when anyone using their services receives more than $600. It's undoubtedly true that some PayPalers are running business payments through the platform and aren't reporting all their income. But it's also true that many people use PayPal for personal purposes. Suppose Shari sends her brother Stuart money for a set of pricey concert tickets he bought on her behalf, then sends him more money to contribute to an upcoming family party. If Shari sent more than $600, PayPal would have to report this to the IRS and Stuart may have to prove to an IRS auditor that the money was for concert tickets and family parties, not some secret business he's running.

I wonder if these new IRS regulations will really stop the rule-breakers. Those who are determined to dodge taxes may, for example, move to crypto currency, leaving the rest of us to deal with the additional IRS paperwork and hassles. I also wonder whether compliance with tax regulations is any better in 2023, when the US Tax Code is 6,871 pages long, with another 68,000 or so pages of regulations, rulings, and tax guidance, than it was in 1773.[15] The tax code was a whole lot slimmer and simpler then, but Bostonians still dumped tea in the harbor to protest taxes!

Strut-Sapper #3 – Not Spreading the News

Yet another way to create resistance to the rules is to neglect explaining them to everyone.

Some organizations invest a fair amount of time and effort when implementing new rules. They'll introduce

---

[15] "How Many Pages Is the Tax Code," Iris.com, https://irisreading.com/how-long-would-it-take-to-read-the-entire-u-s-tax-code/.

them to the workforce before they go into effect, giving people time to learn about them, ask questions, and get adjusted to new routines. Then, once the new rules are introduced, managers will coach employees who have trouble remembering or adapting to the new rules.

Other companies impose new rules with little or no notice, leaving employees feeling as if management cares little about them. In one company I worked with, management sometimes left it up to new field employees to introduce new rules to experienced workers. The new folks learned the new rules in training, then went out to the field to work with experienced employees. An experienced worker, hoping to share her practical experience, might explain something only to have the new employee counter, "We don't do it that way anymore."

"What do you mean?"

"I just went through training, and they said this is the new rule."

If you were the experienced worker, would you be eager to adopt this new rule you just heard about? And would you believe that management, which couldn't be bothered to tell you about the new rule, cared about you?

Strut-Sapper #4 – Too Many, Too Fast

Forcing workers to rapidly adapt to a plethora of new requirements can lead to difficulties. This is a common problem for contractors and subcontractors, who go from site to site and face different sets of written rules and unspoken expectations. The issue can be especially pressing when contractors and subcontractors are working for organizations mature in results, systems, and culture, who expect everyone to align with their understanding of how to approach and perform the work. Contractors and subcontractors who are not used to this degree of maturity will struggle to comply.

Hoping to head off such issues, client organizations often hold contractor summits, bringing together leaders of contractor firms for an open forum, discussing expectations and lessons learned. At one such recent summit, one of the subcontractor leaders shared something to the effect of, "The amount of requirements presented to them to conduct the work is overwhelming. It is creating culture shock. It is so much all at once, and nothing is sticking." This particular client is well known as a constant learning organization, always striving to learn and meet new expectations. If they struggle, what happens with other subcontractors, less mature in their ability to learn and adapt on the spot?

Strut-Sapper #5 – Some Rules that Conflict with Requirements

It's vital to ensure that your rules do not conflict with regulatory requirements or the rules of entities you conduct business with. Failure to do so can create resistance to the rules.

I've seen this happen, for example, with fall safety. Falling is one of the most common causes of serious injuries and fatalities at work. In the United States, OSHA (the Occupational Safety and Health Administration) requires employers to set up the workplace in such a way as to prevent employees from falling off overhead platforms, elevated workstations, and into holes in the floor and walls. The rules require that fall protection be provided at elevations of four feet in general industry workplaces, five feet in shipyards, six feet in the construction industry, and eight feet in longshoring operations.

Many employees use these requirements when creating their safety rules. But other organizations are even more stringent. Most industrial contractors follow OSHA requirements but may find themselves working in client facilities with a 100% requirement, which requires workers to wear fall protection when work is performed at any elevation of one foot or more.

When rules conflict, or worse, feel ridiculous or add no value, people can disengage and begin to question other rules they are exposed to at the workplace.

Strut-Sapper #6 – Neglecting the "Why"

The process of introducing new rules can be difficult, and it sometimes fails. Many people believe this happens because workers resist change. But research has shown that the problem isn't so much that people resist change: it's that that they resist new rules they don't understand. A perfect example of this comes from a European manufacturing company I worked with on safety issues.

Back in 2009, there was a tragic fatality at their plant in northern Italy. Traffic patterns at the facility had recently changed, with large trucks now moving from right to left instead of left to right as they had done for years.

One evening soon after the change, a maintenance technician emerged from between two buildings and onto a road. It was dark, the man was wearing dark clothes, and the facility was very noisy. Tragically, he was struck by a reversing truck and was killed.

The team investigating the terrible accident decided that from now on, all employees at all facilities would be required to wear reflective vests when outdoors. Rather than explaining this new regulation and the reason why it was necessary, the company just said, essentially, "Here's the new policy. Sign this paper indicating you understand it."

The new regulation and papers to sign were sent to every plant, and as expected, the workers resisted. They didn't understand why they had to adopt what to them was a burdensome new rule that made their jobs harder— they'd have to keep track of their vests all day long and made sure they had them in hand when going outside.

I happened to be consulting for this company at the time, and as I went from plant to plant, I learned that the rule was being largely ignored. They only wore the reflective vest at the Italian facility, where many people had known the deceased worker, and at the Irish plant, where only one person had known him.

As it happened, the vice president of engineering at the Ireland plant had been a close friend of the deceased man. The vice president personally introduced the new rule at the Ireland plant, telling the story of what had happened to his friend. He spoke to the workers in small groups, rather than at a mass meeting, and instead of showing them pictures of the accident, he held up pictures of the deceased man's family. He spoke about his friend and told his fellow workers that the new rule would help them avoid a repeat of the terrible tragedy.

Not surprisingly, workers at the Irish plant embraced the new regulation, for the people there knew and embraced the *why*.

I cannot stress enough how vital it is that rules be presented in a way that explains the *why*, addresses the emotions, and obtains worker input to ensure the rules make sense and are understood.

Summing Up the Rules Strut

Rules represent change. Workers must change when they join an organization in order to comply with the existing rules and change again every time new rules are rolled out. Leadership often accuses workers of fighting change, but people don't resist change nearly as much as we think they do. However, as Rick Mauer has pointed out, they do resist the process of change if they (1) don't understand the change, (2) don't like the change, or (3) don't like the person who's bringing the change to them.[16] Items two and three—not liking the change and not liking the person who brings it to them—are emotional responses, and we respond emotionally first before we

---

[16] Rick Mauer, "Resistance to Change – Why it Matters and What to Do About It," *Rick Mauer* (blog), July 5, 2021, https://rickmaurer.com/articles/resistance-to-change-why-it-matters/.

respond logically. This means we have to remember that rules and the process of introducing rules are emotional items, and the emotions must be addressed, not just the logic or process.

So, we can add to the list of items describing the well-made Rules Strut. Ideally, it will:

- assemble all the laws, rules, regulations, guidelines, and expectations relevant to the organization,
- organize and present them in an understandable manner,
- teach the pertinent ones to members of the organization, depending on their needs,
- avoid accountabilism and other strut-sappers, and
- always take emotions into account.

In short, the ideal Rules Strut is a slim and trim organizer and teacher, never to be weighted down with barnacles or other debris.

Enforcing the Rules

As I write this chapter in December of 2022, the actions of Judge Carl Nichols and the 131 other judges who oversaw cases in which they had a financial interest have not yet been examined or reviewed by disciplinary boards. I don't know what actions, if any, such boards may take. But I do know that if a rule isn't enforced, it's as if the rule doesn't exist. It's worse than that, because failure to enforce even a single rule sends a signal that you're not serious about the rule—and if you're not serious about this rule you're probably not serious about other rules.

I had personal experience with enforcement when I was a seventeen-year-old soldier at Fort Gordon, Georgia. Right out of basic training, I had been sent to Fort Gordon for AIT (advanced individual training). Basic had lasted a couple of months, during which time we were locked down at the base. While at AIT we got our first weekend pass, and we were dying to get off base.

A large group of us, young guys and gals, went to a cabin owned by one member of the group for the weekend. When Sunday morning came, we knew we had to be back on the base at a certain time in proper uniform and in formation. We knew that, but some of us took our time and wound up at a Ruby Tuesday's restaurant for what was either a late breakfast or an early lunch; I don't remember what we called it. There were six of us at the restaurant, young men and women trying to squeeze everything we could out of our freedom. But our server, who was familiar with military matters and routines, said to us, "Don't you have to be back at the base soon?"

None of us had a car, and in 1994, Uber hadn't been invented yet. We had to get a cab, but this being our first trip off the base, we didn't know how hard it was to get one in that part of town. We hustled out to find a payphone then called every cab company we found in the phone book. We finally found a couple of cabs— remember, there were six of us—and I wound up hurrying back to base in the backseat of a cab with two women soldiers, all of us dressed in civilian clothing. I was also wearing the cowboy boots I had brought with me to the army, plus a cowboy hat I had just bought in town. I'm from Texas, and I missed wearing my hat and boots during basic.

The cab pulled up right in front of the formation, rows and rows of soldiers in perfect order and proper uniform. Drill Sergeant Martinez looked at me as I got out of the cab, complete with cowboy hat and boots, and said, "Nice of you to join us, now beat your face." That meant I had to do pushups. I started to take off my cowboy hat, but he said, "No, no, you want that cowboy hat so much. Put that cowboy hat back on." So, I had to go down in front of the whole battalion to do my pushups with hat on head. From that point on, all during my AIT stationed at Fort Gordon, I was known as "Private Cowboy."

The Wrong Kind of Enforcement

Rules are not really rules if you don't have to follow them. They must be enforced, and that's what the Enforcement Strut is for. Unfortunately, it can be difficult to construct a good Enforcement Strut. Some organizations err on the side of rigidity, coming down hard on transgressors. Workers comply out of fear, even when they feel that what they've been told to do is foolish, wasteful, or outright dangerous. A certain refinery, which relied on fearful compliance, suffered a terrible accident several decades back. In the transcript of the investigation following the incident, an operator is asked, "Did you know that turning that valve would cause the release which triggered the explosion?"

"Yes."

"Then why did you do it?"

"My boss told me to. I knew it was wrong. But if I didn't do it, I'd get in trouble."

Sometimes workers are resentful rather than fearful and want to vent their feelings. I remember seeing a picture of a gas station in Canada; the photo was taken about twenty years ago. It shows one of those sign boards set outside a business, with letters spelling out messages like "Taco - $3." The sign in this picture said, "My boss told me to change this stupid sign, so I did." This is an example of malicious compliance. In this case, it wasn't too harmful and might have even made some customers laugh. But neither fearful compliance nor malicious compliance will help get your organization to Sustained Excellence. In fact, they'll weaken your Bridge and hold you back.

The Well-Made Enforcement Strut

The Enforcement Strut helps ensure that everyone in the organization complies with all the laws, rules, guidelines, and so on. But it should not just be a punitive, "beat your face" mechanism. Yes, there's a place for strict enforcement of the rules. Some people will have to be disciplined and a few even exited from the organization.

But for the most part, the Enforcement Strut should be built on the understanding that mistakes happen in a complex environment. Even the best of people don't get it right every time in every situation. This means that blaming and shaming is not the ultimate solution, for if you simply blame and shame, you'll get a lot of fearful and malicious compliance, which is not what you want.

Instead, the Enforcement Strut should allow for a generous portion of learning and improving, encouraging everyone to follow the rules for their benefit and for the benefit of all. With this in mind, the well-made Enforcement Strut will:

- lay out a balance of consequences for desired and undesired performance, appropriate for the workplace environment and specific duties,
- hold people accountable for their actions, not just the results, and
- be clear, consistent, and just with enforcement.

In other words, the well-made Enforcement Strut will help shape behavior by acknowledging that, while we are not perfect, we can learn.

Balancing the Consequences

Sometimes you need immediate discipline to extinguish the wrong behavior. In nuclear plants, energy distribution facilities, and other high-danger workplaces, the slightest infraction can lead to disaster. Workers who intentionally or repeatedly break even a single rule may have to be walked out of the workplace and told they are never to return.

But generally speaking, punishment by itself isn't enough, because punishment is a behavior-extinguishing mechanism. It may stop people from doing something— but what will they do instead? Extinguishing unwanted behavior doesn't guarantee the person will suddenly embrace the rules. Instead, they might just get better at not getting caught. Many freeway speeders don't slow down because they get a speeding ticket. They just become better at spotting police cars or hurry over to an electronics store to purchase a radar detector.

Suppose discipline wasn't possible or wasn't a tool you could use in a given situation. What then? All progress begins by thinking differently, so perhaps we need to think differently about how we ensure people follow the rules. And remember that discipline may extinguish an undesirable behavior, but now there's a void. You'd like to fill that void with the desired behavior. To do that, leadership needs to ask itself a two-part question: "What happens if they don't follow the rules, and what happens if they do?"

That is, we know we're going to discipline them if they repeatedly or flagrantly break the rules. But what should we do when they follow the rules? How can we consistently identify, acknowledge, and reinforce the desired behavior?

There is no one-size-fits-all plan for this, for it varies according to the situation. This means that it's up to leadership to balance the consequences, to determine how they will reward desirable behavior as much as they punish undesirable behavior. Some of the ways I've seen include the following:

- A simple and sincere thank you is given.
- Employees are recognized in front of their families.
- COACH coins are given out. So far, this is primarily used in the military but is spreading to many other industries. I have a COACH coin that I occasionally

give to acknowledge great demonstrations of leadership. On the front of the coin it says, "Create Ownership and Change Happens (COACH)™." This was first introduced in my book, *COACH: A Safety Leadership Fable.*

- Hilton has a program, Catch Me at My Best, to identify and recognize employees who do a great job in the eyes of the customer.

In many situations, it doesn't matter what you do so much as workers understand that you see and appreciate their desirable behavior.

Actions Over Results

You don't have to work in a nuclear facility or be a surgeon to find yourself working in a complex environment. Just think about sandwich makers, who must deal with hungry people wanting to eat now, mentally keep track of their orders, listen for the beep of the oven to tell him to take the sandwich out before it dries up, greet customers, ring up orders, remember frequent customers' names, run to the refrigerator in the back room to restock items, and help non-tech-savvy customers use their phones to pay.

Even seemingly simple work can require mastering and juggling various tasks, which is why we must understand the intent behind and influence on a person's actions when things go wrong, not just the results. In addition, leaders must take responsibility. They must ask themselves, "If the employees are not meeting expectations, how effectively are they being led?"

Remember, the goal is to shape behavior. If a behavior led to the wrong results, it may not be the worker's fault. It might be a part of the system the worker works within, or it might be due to the individual being placed in an error-likely situation created by someone or something beyond their control.

When errors occur, it's best to identify the influences on actions and to avoid the poor leadership approaches of naming, blaming, shaming, and retraining. Always remember that some of these error-likely situations are caused by imprecise communication, insufficient training, inexperienced workers being placed in situations better suited to experienced workers, and proper tools or personal protective equipment not being readily available. In other words, they're caused by problems with leadership.

Enforcement is about shaping performance, about ensuring that the desired performance and outcomes are consistently occurring. Sometimes, accomplishing this means shaping leadership's behavior.

Conflicting Messages Make a Mockery of . . . Everything!

Even with the best of intentions, leaders sometimes give out conflicting messages that influence decision-making.

An oil company I once worked with seemed to have a great attitude toward safety. The organization's Senior Vice President of Operations had a favorite saying which was something like, "This oil has been in the ground for a million years, so we don't have to rush and take risks to get it out today."

That seems to be a strong, clear statement that leadership values worker safety over production, that it's more important to ensure everyone is safe than it is to fulfill the daily, monthly, quarterly, and yearly production quotas.

Yet workers were constantly being pushed by functional leaders in other departments to hurry up. They were pressured to complete additional stages of drilling to meet schedules, to get that oil out of the ground as soon as possible!

One part of leadership was telling them to be safe while another part, closer to them, was telling them to hurry, even though hurrying required them to take risks. These sorts of dueling dictates destroy workers' trust in leadership and management, disrupt teamwork, and otherwise take a buzzsaw to the Bridge.

Rules Plus Enforcement

Enforcement should always work hand in hand with the rules, which means that shaping behavior begins by shaping the rules.

Ideally, there is no separation between rules and enforcement. Workers will see the rules as helpful and will encourage fellow workers to follow the rules for everyone's benefit. The rules will be self-enforcing, and management can focus on helping everyone get even better at what they do.

Unfortunately, the ideal is a difficult state to achieve. We must face the real-world reality that we are often barnacled with useless, redundant, and cumbersome rules that get in the workers' way, cause confusion and upset, and strain relations between management and workers. We also have to face the reality that not all workers will follow the rules. This may be because management or leadership is giving mixed signals, because the workers are poorly suited for their particular duties, because outside pressures are distracting the workers, or because of a lack of alignment within leadership, leading to conflicting direction and priorities.

Given all this, it's clear that we need to enforce the rules. This may be especially true in organizations that have undergone significant changes in leadership, workforce, strategy, market conditions, or other situations. Such organizations may be forced to spend a lot of time teaching and enforcing the rules, with little time or energy left over for shaping behavior.

And sometimes the ax must fall. I know of one organization that instituted a policy saying that you could not use a mobile device while driving on company property. Months after the policy was implemented, a senior executive was seen using a cell phone while driving in the company parking lot. He was quickly exited from the organization. As a result, everyone could see that leadership was serious about this rule, and if they hadn't yet adjusted their behavior, they had plenty of incentive to do so immediately.

Other organizations conduct show-me audits, asking employees to demonstrate a procedure or series of procedures to assess their competency and adherence to standardized practices. If undesired behavior is identified, rather than punishing, they coach workers who are not up to snuff. And workers who do pass the audit are acknowledged. This is a good example of enforcement designed to improve behavior and get better results rather than blaming and shaming.

Summing Up: Rules and Enforcement, Hand in Hand

Leadership's goal is to create a streamlined, well-reasoned set of rules that helps workers excel and to enforce these rules in a way that helps workers and the organization improve in every way. Rules should be viewed as helpful guides to excellence rather than as "punishment triggers," while enforcement should be viewed as a means to improvement, not a penalty.

For the sake of clarity, the Rules Strut and Enforcement Strut are shown as separate pieces on the Bridge. But they are really complementary, interlacing paths to excellence.

This is a key point: We should not think of rules and enforcement as being crime and punishment. Rules and enforcement should be understood as being one and the same in purpose and intent, both designed to help workers acquire the individual excellence that makes for organizational excellence.

When we do this, we free up the Enforcement Strut to concentrate on helping to shape the behavior that makes for excellence. Yes, discipline must always be there. It gives those who need it an incentive to learn and stay on course and helps weed out those who cannot or will not comply with the rules. So, while discipline is always a part of enforcement, the bulk of the Enforcement Strut should be devoted to teaching, coaching, correcting, and motivating people to be their best, for their own sake and for the betterment of the organization.

Insights from Industry Leaders

I asked leaders from a number of industries—including for-profit, non-profit, and governmental—for their insights into rules and enforcement.

With respect to rules, I asked: What are the most important (significant few) rules you need your employees or personnel to follow?

Here are some of their answers:

Mark Kehne, plant manager, Cardinal FG

- Our significant rules are presented as six fundamental expectations for all employees:
  - Safe Production is our highest priority.
  - Perform your job in the manner in which you were trained, never attempt to perform a task for which you have not been trained, and *never* skip steps.
  - Abide by all plant procedures and policies.
  - Be fully present.
  - Be a positive influence on your team.
  - Maintain the highest of housekeeping standards.

Tobias Read, founder, AQRA Group

- The obligation to dissent and the security that you can dissent with impunity—as it relates to providing feedback, highlighting issues or simply making suggestions—assuming, of course, this is done with professionalism.

Michael J. Devane, vice president of operations, CertainTeed

- We have a set of "principles of conduct" that I find to be extremely valuable in talking with my plant teams. These are my takeaways:
  1. Professional commitment – what we all have in common; mobilizing the best of my ability; commitment, willingness, what I do well, and I train myself to do better; conscious of my actions' impact; and assuring caring for the environment and worker health and safety.
  2. Respect for others – acceptance of pluralism; personal development of each person; ready to listen to others, other cultures, backgrounds, religions, countries, and so on; don't embarrass your colleagues or business partners; giving time is showing respect.
  3. Integrity – requires rigorous adherence to probity (the quality of having strong moral principles; honesty and decency) in all professional activities; no individual may compromise the interests of the group entrusted to them in favor of their own personal interests; detailed rules of

engagement for certain categories of group personnel.

4. Loyalty – the respect that we owe the group that employs us; honesty and fairness with superiors, employees and colleagues and customers, suppliers, and any business partners; and respect for the guidelines and internal rules.

5. Solidarity – responsibility at work; teamwork; and bringing out the best in each person.

Chris Boleman, president and chief executive officer, Houston Livestock Show and Rodeo

- Be accountable to yourself, your team, and the organization. If everyone is accountable and does their part, the work gets done.
- Create space to be creative. We tend to get caught up in how we have always done it. It is important to be purposeful in allowing people to be creative. Even if the idea isn't adopted, there is something to be said for discussing new ideas and being open to change. Often, an idea may not be "ripe," but eventually it will happen when the time is right.
- Respect each other. Each one of us brings different perspectives, views things through different lenses, and frankly just sees things differently. Everyone has value even though their ideas might be different than yours. Everyone should be respected and be able to share these ideas in a safe, open environment.

Joel Simon, partner, Fernelius and Simon

- The most important rule I have is that if there is a problem, I want to hear about it first from my employees. Mistakes, errors, and problems will happen. It is how one responds to mistakes, errors, and problems that defines success.

Najya Al Hinai, continuous improvement lead, MSEML

- There are three main fundamental golden rules we go by. They are (1) intervene, (2) comply, and (3) respect. By applying these three rules to our day-to-day business, we encourage staff to intervene by challenging the status quo or when they see something unsafe, which allows opportunities for learning, pivoting, and experimentation. The second rule is to comply, be it to regulations, lifesaving rules, or company policy, and procedures. The third rule is respect. It is important that we conduct ourselves respectfully to each other, our contractors, our stakeholders, and our community.

With respect to enforcement, I asked: What does good enforcement of the rules look like in practice?

Here are some of their answers:

Mark Kehne, plant manager, Cardinal FG

- Ours is an organization that promotes a coaching approach to rule enforcement. Coaching skills are included in training for all new employees at all levels. The best demonstration of enforcement of the rules is when coworkers coach one another on best practices. The objective of rules enforcement is to correct behaviors, and discipline is only utilized when coaching has failed or when a violation is egregious, repeated, or presents a significant risk.

Kelvin E. Roth, vice president, environmental, health, safety, and quality, CF Industries

- Enforcement to me is about accountability. Safety processes should be mutual agreements—both sides understand expectations of process. When those expectations are broken, that's where enforcement comes in. But it should be a last resort and limited to cases of clear disregard. I'm not a fan of cardinal rules, as they imply two things: (1) this is more important than any other safety practice or precaution and (2) our systems are so good that the only reason for not meeting expectations falls on the individual.

Michael J. Devane, vice president of operations, CertainTeed

- First, make clear the rules of engagement and the consequences of failing to follow them. I think this is basic respect for employees that is sometimes forgotten. Once this is in place, it is all about clear communication in real time of instances of recognition as well as improvement. I approach my team with the attitude that I want to help them get to the career development point that they want, and with that support comes very direct and constructive feedback in real time. My intentions are always positive in the sense that I am attempting to help them improve.

Chris Boleman, president and chief executive officer, Houston Livestock Show and Rodeo

- There has to be a structured evaluation methodology in an organization. Enforcement should match agreed-upon employee goals, and these goals *must* align with the organizational strategic plan.
- In addition to structured evaluations, enforcement must be in the moment or shortly thereafter. Not addressing issues or problems results in the accepted behavior causing uncertainty on teams.

Kirk Bagnal, owner, Ethostory

- One of the five human performance improvement principles (HPIP) developed by the US Department of Energy in response to the "Three-Mile Island Nuclear Incident" states, "People achieve high levels of performance based largely on the encouragement and reinforcement received from leaders, peers, and subordinates." This fourth HPIP answers the question of what enforcement of rules truly looks like in practice. It involves positional leaders influencing people to influence their peers to adhere to the few (but important) established rules. If we consider Steven Covey's circles of control, influence, and concern (working from the inside smallest circle outward), we, as leaders, need to focus our efforts on influencing the most influential people in our organization to adhere to, apply, and enforce the rules. Otherwise, we, as positional leaders, will turn into a constant policing organization—literally and unintentionally becoming a police force rather than a resource for our people. With that being said, it is still our responsibility to *always* confront something that does not meet our standard. Now, we should apply wisdom and context to each situation. Varying responses are required in different situations, but a response is always required. Remember, when we—once again, as *leaders*—walk by something that does not align with the rules or standards, we are sanctioning it to happen again and again. One additional item to note is embedded in that HPIP: the word *encouragement*. Not only must we confront what is wrong; we have an opportunity, a responsibility, and an obligation to encourage what is right. If we can move the needle further toward encouragement and away from ignoring, we will build a transparent and just culture where rule enforcement is not as necessary.

Joel Simon, partner, Fernelius and Simon

- Consistency. Personally, I never demand anything of any employee that I would not be willing to do myself. Culture starts at the top. If I expect an employee to follow a rule, that rule also applies to me and every other employee equally.

Najya Al Hinai, continuous improvement lead, MSEML

- The rules must first be stated clearly, communicated continuously, and be easily available for reference. Employees must be made aware of the rules that apply specifically to them, depending on their line of work. Before rules can be enforced, the organization must ensure those rules can be applied through upskilling and training, with resources and budget to comply.

Additionally, there must be means to audit and assure compliance, with the opportunity for those in the frontline to feedback into the plan, do, check, act (PDCA) loop.

Commander Richard H. Tetrev, US Navy (retired)

- Your unit, being great or small, is focused on one goal: keeping all citizens of our country safe and free. For this to happen, everyone must understand and know their duties, practice them with honor (no corners cut, always supporting the other members of the team, be honest with themselves and others), and be totally focused on the one goal.

Michael Middleton, safety and health director, Georgia Power

- To me, good enforcement is an attempt to maintain a consistent balance between accountability and learning. The challenge is the subjectivity and the inherent biases that exist in driving toward what is fair. "Fair" is a moving target and can quickly erode your culture if it's not managed. As a leader of an organization, what you do to and how you go about establishing trust is critical. Hiring competent leaders who are trustworthy and can enforce and support the established rules of the organization is instrumental to the success of the enterprise.

Key Points about Rules and Enforcement

- Ideally, the Rules Strut organizes, presents, and teaches the rules in such a way that makes compliance understandable, agreeable, and easy and in so doing, enhances production, customer service, and everything else the organization does.

- There are numerous ways to damage the Rules Strut, including having too many rules, accountabilism, having rules that conflict with regulatory requirements, properly explaining the rules, and not taking emotions into account.

- Rules are not really rules if you don't have to follow them.

- The Enforcement Strut should be built on the understanding that mistakes happen in a complex environment and must allow for a generous portion of learning and improving.

- There should be a balance of consequences to shape behavior based on two questions: what happens if they follow the rules, and what happens if they do not?

- When things go wrong, we must try to understand the intent behind and influence on a person's actions, not just the results.

- We should not think of rules and enforcement as being crime and punishment. Rules and enforcement should be understood as being one and the same, in purpose and intent, with both designed to help workers acquire the individual excellence that makes for organizational excellence.

Questions to Consider

1. On a scale of one to ten, with one indicating you have yet to begin and ten that you are great, how would you rate the effectiveness and completeness of the rules element of your organization's Bridge?

2. What should be done to improve the clarity of and compliance with the rules within your organization?

3. On the same scale of one to ten, how would you rate the effectiveness of the enforcement element of your organization's Bridge?

4. What should be done to improve the effectiveness of enforcement within your organization?

Chapter Six – Culture and Workers

In AD 73, two organizations with powerful but very different cultures clashed in a barren Middle East desert. Huddled in a fortress atop a mesa in the Judean Desert in what is now Israel were some 970 Zealots, members of a Jewish sect that strongly believed in the God of Israel and refused to change their beliefs or practices, not an iota. This brought them into conflict with the Roman Empire, which controlled much of the Middle East and had a much different approach to religion, including praying to numerous gods. After many years of tension over religion and other issues, the Zealots launched a rebellion that became known as the First Jewish-Roman War. The rebels destroyed an entire Roman legion and captured Jerusalem and a great deal of other territory, including the mountaintop fortress of Masada in the Judean desert.

Although the Zealots were determined, they were no match for the Roman war machine and were methodically beaten back by the Romans, whose ability to absorb loss after loss yet press ahead had allowed them to conquer much of Europe, Northern Africa, and the Middle East. As the war came to an end, the only remaining Jewish stronghold was Masada, where less than a thousand Zealots, including women and children, hoped they could simply wait until the Romans got tired and left.

But where others would have seen the impossibly steep slopes of the mountain atop which Masada perched as being impossible for armed soldiers to scale and the fortress walls atop the mountain as being too difficult to bring down, to the Romans this was simply another engineering problem to be solved. Ignoring the blazing sun, the Roman Tenth Legion built a camp at the base of the mountain, constructed a seven-mile-long siege wall at the base of the mountain, and then began piling stones upon stones, filling the gaps with dirt. For over a year, some fourteen thousand soldiers and slaves toiled away. After digging a mountain of stone and dirt out of the ground and piling it high, they had created what amounted to a second mountain, butted up against the mountain of Masada. The Romans used their "mountain," which had a sloping side, to push siege machines up to the Zealot fortress, whose walls they quickly breached.

But the next day, when the Romans launched their final assault into the broken walls, they found that rather than surrender and be killed or sold into slavery, the Zealots had committed mass suicide. Only seven were still alive, two women and five children who had hidden in a water conduit and had witnessed firsthand the incredible power of organizational culture.

For that is what the Zealots and Roman Army were, organizations with incredibly powerful cultures. The Zealot organization was smaller, loosely organized, and dependent on inspirational leadership, while the Roman Army organization was larger, well organized, and hierarchically structured. One culture sprang from a conversation between God and the prophet Abraham, the other from a fight between the brothers Romulus and Remus. One culture was inward looking, the other very assertive and acquisitive. One culture believed that if it worshiped and behaved in the proper manner, it would be favored and protected by the one true God, while the other believed that propitiating numerous gods would guarantee success.

The Zealot and Roman Army organizations were different in every way except one: they were driven by powerful organizational culture. Each culture was focused on success, although they interpreted success differently. The Zealot definition of success compelled them to die rather than abandon their faith, while the Roman Army definition of success allowed them to sacrifice a great many lives and resources, plus a great deal of time, rather than to fail.

The Ever-Present Unseen

Culture is the driving force for every organization. It defines the organization and determines the direction it takes, the force of its movement, and its attitudes toward itself, its customers or clients, the law, and everything else.

Every organization has a culture, whether it be a business, army, NGO, church, rugby team, or what have you. Even amorphous organizations like rebellions and loosely organized sects have cultures. As soon as two people come together to form an organization, you have the beginnings of a culture. As more and more people join and the organization is forced to deal with more external factors—such as OSHA, competition, and the expectations of financiers—the culture becomes more complex. Indeed, rather than a single, identifiable culture, a large organization may have different cultures in different parts of the organization. These cultures may compete and clash, interfere with and undermine each other, resist all efforts by the leader to get them under control, and eventually destroy the organization.

Culture is present and powerful in every organization. You can't hide from culture, and you can't hide it away.

Where Does Culture Come From?

Culture springs from the perceptions and behaviors that exist within an organization and the way those behaviors are reinforced—or not. Let's look at culture from the safety point of view by imagining that Iza Newhire is beginning her new job in a factory. Iza has certain perceptions about work and safety made up of her personal ideas and previous work experience. She carries these perceptions, these beliefs, with her into the new job.

Iza, who is assigned to work at a certain machine, believes that safety comes first. That's what the bosses at her old job told her, and that's what her new bosses emphasized during the onboarding process. But during her first week at the new job, she hears a story about an employee named Steven who stopped his machine because of a safety issue. That's what he had been told to do, but his supervisor scolded him for doing so. Then, the story goes, Steven was passed over for promotion, reassigned to a crappy job, and wound up leaving the company.

After hearing this story, Iza is wondering if her perception about safety coming first is correct. Still, when a major safety issue pops up at her machine one morning, she hits the stop button. Almost immediately the shift supervisor hurries over, restarts the machine, and pulls Iza aside to ask her why she stopped the machine. The supervisor doesn't actually dress Iza down, but he does stress that her machine has to produce X number of units per hour, and they can't afford any unscheduled down time.

Iza goes back to work at her machine, but warily so. She's not sure the machine is trustworthy, so she works very carefully and doesn't produce enough units per hour. She's worried about being scolded for failing to make her production number—that would be her second scolding in one day. During her lunch break she finds herself seated at a table with the fellow who had told her the story of Steven. Iza tells him about her own experience and soon, the story of Steven has been enlarged to include Iza's negative experience and is passed around the entire factory floor.

The organization's culture has changed, slightly, for now there's one more piece of evidence that management doesn't really care about safety, that only production matters. As a result, workers feel more inclined to bend or ignore safety rules because they believe they are rated according to production, not safety compliance, no matter what management claims. And they're afraid to stop production over safety issues, even serious ones, so they're on edge when their machines start acting up. They have less respect for and trust in management because they perceive that management doesn't care if a worker loses a finger or worse as long as those units keep rolling off the machines.

This little tale of Iza Newhire illustrates how organizational culture is formed and normed. It was about safety, but it applies to all aspects of an organization, from housekeeping to customer service, quality to productivity.

As you can see, culture begins with the existing perceptions within an organization. Whether the organization is one day old or one hundred years old, whether it's a small shop or a multinational corporation with dozens of locations across the globe, it has a set of perceptions—or maybe numerous sets, creating silos throughout the organization.

These perceptions effect everyone's attitudes toward the organization, their work, their desire to provide discretionary effort, and more. The attitudes may be positive, as in, "This organization really cares about safety," or negative, as in, "The company cares more about units out the door than it does me."

Over time, management reinforces attitudes by rewarding or punishing certain behaviors, such as praising or scolding someone for stopping their machine over a safety concern. These rewards and punishments either confirm existing workers' values or create new ones. Workers will learn to value, for example, getting units out the door over safety, or keeping silent about mistakes rather than speaking up when things do not seem right.

This is an important point, so it's worth a bit of elaboration. Values are created when behaviors are reinforced at or near the point of decision. The point of decision is the moment when a worker has to make a choice. For example, stop the machine, or let it run? Push the customer to buy more than he needs, or sell him what he asked for? Stop to assist a coworker, or ignore her? Review the spreadsheet one more time, or just send it in?

Reinforcing behaviors at or near the point of decision creates values. Over time, these values affect decisions, which are reflected in the things people say and do, as in letting the dangerous machine run and telling new hires to ignore what the bosses say about safety.

As the values spread and become the norm, the decisions they trigger become "the way we do things around here." But note that culture is not "the way we do things around here." Culture is the reason why we do those things.

In our story, Iza Newhire began with the perception that safety was paramount and had the attitude that "this company cares about safety." But when she was scolded for making a decision (turning off the machine), her perception and attitude shifted. She learned to value production over all else, and when safety issues arose, she decided to ignore them. Her new norm became "keep the machines running no matter what." She, like everyone else in this imaginary factory, now values production first. They've also learned to value keeping the boss happy, so they don't mention little problems with the machines—not until they become huge problems that can't be ignored and work grinds to a halt. But, hey, that's the way we do things around here!

So, this is the culture-building algorithm: perceptions → attitudes → reinforcement → behaviors → values → decisions = the way we do things around here. This algorithm runs forever, over and over again, changing every time perceptions, attitudes, reinforcement, behaviors, values, and/or decisions are changed, even slightly. And the entire never-ending sequence is reinforced by expectations, experiences, and storytelling.

Suppose when she begins working in the factory, Iza expects that she will be thanked for stopping her machine over safety concerns. If she is indeed thanked for stopping the machine, her expectation is in line with her experience. Because her expectation and experience are aligned, that is, because she had a good experience when she stopped the line, she won't say much about the incident to her fellow workers. Why should she, when everyone knows that's what was supposed to happen? There's no story here.

Now suppose that her experience was more positive than she expected—perhaps the factory manager personally thanked her for stopping the misbehaving machine. Her expectation has been exceeded, and she's got a little story to tell. She'll mention what happened to a few fellow workers, and it will have a small effect on the culture, reinforcing it in a positive manner.

But let's suppose Iza's expectations were crushed because she was scolded. Now she's got a big story to tell and will broadcast what happened to more than a few of her friends. The more undesirable her experience and the more it deviated from her expectations in a negative manner, the louder and longer she'll tell her tale of woe. And the more she talks about it, the more others will pick up on it and spread it around.

As you can see, culture is created and either maintained or reshaped by the constant interplay of perceptions, attitudes, reinforcements, behaviors, values, decisions, expectations, experiences, and stories. Leadership does not create culture, but neither is it a prisoner of culture. Leaders can influence culture by influencing perceptions, and they do that by managing the experiences that shape the perceptions that drive the storytelling that influences the culture. Creating the right experiences will shape the storytelling, that will confirm the perceptions you want people to have.

Storytelling is a crucial part of culture-building, so long as the stories told match the reality on the floor. Imagine that you're a new hire, and you're told about an employee who was rewarded for identifying continuous improvement opportunities and participating in the intervention. Or you're told the story of an employee who worked behind the scenes to help find consensus between labor and salaried leadership moments before going into a union contract negotiation.

These stories will create a strong impression on you and will go a long way toward setting the perceptions, expectations, and experiences that lead to great organizational culture.

This is a key point: group behaviors do not create organizational culture but are a result of the culture. And culture doesn't pull an organization down. The organization pulls the culture down by allowing or even encouraging, deliberately or not, a mismatch between perceptions, expectations, and experiences by allowing the resulting storytelling to change perceptions and pull the organization down the wrong path.

Just remember how powerful the "story we tell ourselves" was to both the Zealot organization and the Roman organization.

What Great Organizational Culture Looks Like

The definition of superior culture varies from organization to organization, industry to industry, activity to activity, and region to region, and it evolves over time. In medieval Europe, apprentices in a master blacksmith's workshop might have felt the culture was great if they were well fed and not physically beaten. They were perfectly content to work what we would today consider brutally long hours, inhale noxious odors all day long, and sleep on the floor.

In late eighteenth and early nineteenth centuries England, many farmers who could no longer feed their families were forced to take industrial jobs in the city, working six long days a week in unheated factories where workers were regularly injured, sometimes horribly so. They might have felt the culture was fine because they were paid every week and their families could eat.

During World War II, many Japanese soldiers and airmen willingly gave their lives in suicidal banzai charges and kamikaze airplane crashes for the greater glory of the emperor, whom they believed to be a descendent of the gods.

My point is not to criticize or defend any organizational culture but simply to point out that there is no single definition of great culture that can apply to all organizations everywhere across time. However, there are some general principles that apply to most organizations in most of today's advanced economies wishing to develop a superior culture. Such a culture would be based on the following:

- Ensure that all necessary rules and regulations are complied with.
- Acknowledge and accept the fact that people make mistakes.
- Understand that you can't prevent all undesirable things from happening, but you can learn to recognize and manage situations in which errors are likely.
- Understand that where there is ownership, there is engagement.
- Purposefully seek out expertise where it exists in the business, prior to making decisions that affect the workforce.
- Understand that people respond emotionally to change before they respond intellectually.
- Understand that coaching produces better performance than does policing.
- Inspire workers to voluntarily go the extra mile to ensure the success of the organization because they want to, not because they have to.

Putting Their Money Where Their Culture Is

Some companies go to great lengths to ensure that new hires will fit into their existing culture. Under its late CEO Tony Hseih, the shoe company Zappos offered new hires $2,000 to quit a few weeks after being hired. This was because Hseih only wanted people who truly believed in the Zappos ethos and were eager to work there because of the culture and not just for the paycheck. This approach has been picked up by other companies, including a software outfit called Trainual. Despite the fact that many organizations have had trouble finding staff during the "Great Resignation" and "quiet quitting," Trainual offers new hires $5,000 to quit if they don't feel they are a perfect fit with Trainual and its culture after just two weeks.[17]

Toyota has a different, equally powerful, approach. When they build a new plant, before they start work, they bring together the people who will work in that facility to create the expectations, build teamwork, and inculcate the culture. The goal is to get everyone onboard with the culture before anyone steps up to the assembly line.

The Worker-Culture Continuum

As you'll notice in Diagram 4 the Worker Tower sits right atop the Culture Pillar on the Bridge to Excellence. This is because culture cannot exist without workers, and workers cannot come together without there being a

---

[17] Danielle Wallace, "Arizona CEO's Answer to 'Great Resignation' Is Offering $5k Bonuses for New Hires to Quit," *FOX Business*, January 9, 2022, https://www.foxbusiness.com/lifestyle/arizona-ceo-great-resignation-pay-to-quit-bonuses.

culture. So, as you create your Bridge, remember that the Culture Pillar and the Workers Tower are not separate and independent. Instead, they are in many ways one and the same, different ways of understanding and approaching the same idea.

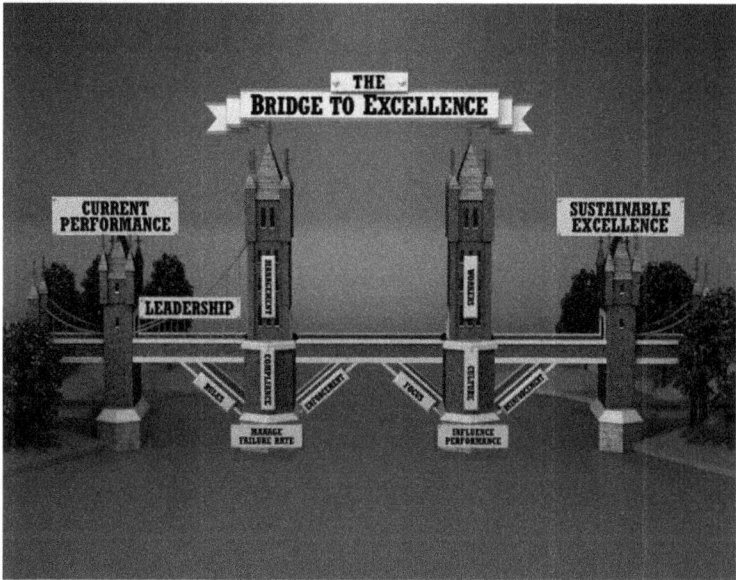

Diagram 4: Workers, Culture, Focus and Reinforcement

Because Workers and Culture are so tightly joined, the words and actions of management and leadership matter. Every single word, every single action, matters greatly. Collectively, they matter more than strategy, more than training, and even more than the best executed plan. That's because the words and actions of management and leadership, acting through the Workers Tower, become the organizational culture. These words and actions can create culture from scratch, change it over time, and if the words and actions are misaligned or harmful, destroy it.

Remember, workers are not the culture and do not create the culture. Instead, they are the conduit to culture, and then they become exemplars of the culture. That is, the workers hear and see the words and actions of management and leadership; absorb, interpret, and perhaps amend these words and actions; then internalize and act them out.

This means that workers cannot be blamed for the culture, for they did not create it. It also means that culture cannot be created in the abstract or by orders from on high. Nevertheless, many organizations try to do just that. They create catchy cultural slogans, run workers through seminars designed to inculcate this culture, and hang colorful culture-reminding posters in various places. Most of these organizations are sincere in their efforts; they genuinely want to have what they consider to be great culture. But they fail when they don't follow through by ensuring that all their words and actions support and reinforce that culture. When management and leadership see culture as just another program to impose upon the workers, yet another box to check off a list, they cannot possibly say the words and perform the actions that will lead to the creation of the desired experiences and stories that create and amend culture.

For management and leadership to truly believe in what they say and do, they must understand that they are part of the Workers Tower; they are part of the workforce and part of the Workers-Culture continuum.

We normally think of workers as being the ones who produce the organization's goods or services as opposed to management and leadership. But that's a limited way of viewing things, for leadership only exists to lead the production of those goods or services, and management only exists to manage that production. Everyone in the organization is there to produce those goods or services, contributing in their own way. This means, for the purposes of the Bridge to Excellence, that everyone is a worker. The CEO is as much a worker as the people digging trenches to lay underground pipes, running machines, interacting with customers, handling paperwork, or dealing with governmental licenses and contract issues.

When building your Bridge to Excellence, remember that everyone in your organization is a part of the Workers Pillar. This is key, because if you see yourself as being apart from the Workers Pillar, as someone who shapes culture rather than is a part of culture, you cannot help but feel that culture is a thing to impose on others. It's for them, not you. Your words will grate on the workers, and your actions will prove to them that you are insincere. At best they will tolerate you because they need a paycheck. At worst, they will deliberately undermine your efforts.

It's only when you see yourself as belonging to the Workers Pillar and understand that you are part of a never-ending cycle of culture creation that your words and actions can be in harmony with the culture you wish to create. This requires a shift in thinking. It requires everyone in the organization to understand that they are all contributing to the creation of the organization's product or service in different ways and that everyone is part of the combined Workers Tower and Culture Pillar.

Many companies look for fit when hiring workers, hoping to find those who will work well with the existing culture. That's well and good, but perhaps they should consider adding another step: when hiring for leadership and management, look for those who understand the powerful impact they have on organizational culture and who see themselves as belonging to the workers-culture continuum.

Culture Matters

For years, Seattle-based Boeing worked to maintain a culture where it was safe to discuss all things regarding safety, not just the safety of the workers building its airplanes but the safety of passengers as well. With a well-deserved reputation for producing safe planes, Boeing was profitable for years. Then the times changed, competition arose from a European manufacturer, and Boeing was merged with another company, one more focused on profits.

The other company's leadership took control of the combined organization, and they were very concerned with the quarterly review, stock price, and other financial matters. They promoted certain people and rewarded certain behaviors and decisions in such a way as to shift the culture away from a preoccupation with safety, away from a culture of speaking up when there were concerns. The new culture gave prominence to production and profits, and soon enough it wasn't so safe to discuss all things safety. It also wasn't safe to discuss items across departments. Even if you wanted to, it was difficult, for leadership had moved itself to Chicago, half a continent away from the engineers who designed the planes and worried about their safety. The move happened in 2001. In 2018 and 2019, Boeing's 737 Max suffered two fatal crashes.

The problem was a lack of a back-up sensor on the nose of the 737 airplane. Back-up instrumentation is standard on airplanes, and Boeing engineers were well aware of the potential for problems should the sole sensor fail. But the culture had changed, and engineers were no longer comfortable hitting the stop button on projects.

One set of Boeing's leaders cultivated a culture where safety was prized, and a later set of leaders shifted that culture to prize profits. Profits are important, of course, but it's hard to profit when your products are literally crashing and killing people. Unfortunately, this problem is common. Cultural attitudes and conflicts were behind the Bhopal, Challenger, Chernobyl, and Deepwater Horizon tragedies and many others.

What you as a leader say and do really matters because it shapes the *why* which drives the culture, which drives worker decision-making that becomes "the way we do things around here."

Insights from Industry Leaders

I asked leaders from a number of industries—including for-profit, non-profit, and governmental—for their insights into culture and workers.

With respect to culture, I asked, What are the most critical considerations for company culture?

Here is an interesting answer:

Kelvin E. Roth, vice president, environmental, health, safety, and quality, CF Industries

- Walk the talk! All companies have values and nearly all of them are good. But do they meet or intend to meet those values? That's what employees watch closely and then adjust their behavior accordingly.

With respect to workers, I asked: What do you look for when hiring and adding to your team?

Here is an interesting answer:

Kolin Ibrahim, senior manager, environmental, health, and safety, Hess Corporation

- Integrity
- Intelligence
- Maturity
- Positive energy, passion
- Ability to energize others
- Edge – can make and take tough decisions
- The ability to execute
- Diversity – equity and equality

Key Points about Culture and Workers

- Culture is the driving force for every organization. It defines the organization and determines the direction it takes, the force of its movement, as well as its attitudes toward itself, its customers or clients, the law, and everything else.
- Culture is not "the way we do things around here." Culture is the reason why we do those things.
- Culture is present and powerful in every organization. You can't hide from culture, and you can't hide it away.
- Group behaviors do not create organizational culture; they are a result of the culture.
- Values are created when behaviors are reinforced at or near the point of decision.

Questions to Consider

1. What is your confidence with your cultural capacity to norm desired beliefs, behaviors, and experiences with existing and new employees?
2. On a scale of one to ten, with one indicating you have yet to begin and ten that you are great, how would you rate the effectiveness of your organization's culture?
3. What, if improved, would add value to your efforts to improve your organizational culture?
4. On the same scale of one to ten, what score would you give for the level of workforce engagement throughout the organization?

Chapter Seven – Focus and Reinforcement

If you live in the Houston area, as I do, you quickly become all too familiar with roadside debris and the problems it causes. It seems as if there's always some major road being repaired, with lots of little rocks and other construction rubble on the roadside. Despite the best efforts of the road crews, some of this gets on the road, is kicked up by the tires of vehicles flying by, and smacks into the windshields of other cars. If you drive in Houston, sooner or later you'll be calling a windshield repair company.

One of the major US windshield repair companies is Safelite, which in 2012 was a $1 billion enterprise with a heavy emphasis on operations. At that time, CEO Tom Feeney was pleased with the growth the company had enjoyed over the past several years but was concerned about the future. He wondered what direction to take in the coming years, what to focus on. He could have continued to zero in on operations, which had been a big driver of Safelite's growth. He could have chosen to focus on the technology of windshields. (A windshield isn't just curved glass. Certain advanced systems in modern cars, such as collision avoidance and lane tracking, are either projected on to the windshield or pass through it.) That focus would also have made sense, what with the continued technologization of cars and trucks. And there were other options.

But Feeney decided to put the company's energies onto becoming a customer-driven organization, to focus on making their customers happy. Shifting from an operations focus to a customer focus wasn't easy. Among other things, the company had to do the following:

- Create a statement of purpose that directed everyone's attention to the goal: "We exist to make a difference and bring unexpected happiness to people's everyday lives."
- Draw up the "Safelite Spirit," which encouraged employees to develop a service mindset, can-do spirit, and caring heart.
- Start listening to what customers were saying rather than relying on statistical metrics.
- Revamp their website, making it much easier for customers to give the company their insurance and other information and schedule appointments to get their windshields replaced. (They reduced the number of clicks required from forty down to fifteen.)
- Begin rating employees for their ability to embrace the new program.

These helped get everyone at Safelite focused on the goal of bringing "unexpected happiness" to their customers—and to remain focused on the goal, even when the boss wasn't looking.

The shift from an operations orientation to a customer orientation took about five years, and when it was complete, customers were indeed much happier and revenue doubled. By focusing on and becoming great at one thing, Safelite improved in other areas as well—without specifically trying to.

In chapter four, we talked about compliance, which is what people in the organization *have* to do. Indeed, the entire first half of the Bridge to Excellence is built on compliance, on keeping the organization up and running.

Now we turn to the Focus and Reinforcement struts, which tie the Culture Pillar to the Bridge's roadbed. While compliance is concerned with what *must* be done, focus and reinforcement look at what people in the organization *want* to do. And when you move from what workers *have* to do to what they *want* to do, you can move from staying alive to thriving.

An easy way to understand focus and reinforcement is to ask yourself these questions:

- What are those handful of things that, if we do them well, will help us become great?
- How do we get our people to pay close attention to certain things as a matter of routine, as well as a matter of great personal importance?
- How do we reinforce the beliefs and behaviors we want everyone to adopt?

In other words, how do we get people to want to do the things that will make us great because doing so matters to them personally? And how do we know which specific few things will put teams, areas, shifts, departments, facilities, or the entire organization on the path to greatness?

Everybody in an organization must pay attention to something, sometimes many things, just to get through the workday. Whether it's repairing bicycles, delivering babies, soothing upset customers, or trying to unsnarl the supply chain, everyone has assigned tasks that must be performed, often in a carefully prescribed manner.

But everybody also has some time, even if only a few moments, in which to make their own decisions. The grocery clerk can decide to greet a customer or to jump right into scanning. The physician can push through the series of questions that must be asked, eyes firmly glued to the keyboard as they enter the patient's responses, or decide to look up and take a few moments to interact with the patient as a person. The supervisor can decide to stop and acknowledge a worker for demonstrating the right spirit or just move on. The machine operator can decide to investigate that slight noise or not.

It's these little moments, these hundreds or thousands of moments every day, that help determine whether your organization will be adequate or great. No matter how carefully you script and restrict your workers' actions, no matter how many checklists they must follow and metrics they must meet, there will be moments where they make decisions.

These are the moments that you, the leader, must master as you move onto the second half of the Bridge and then beyond to Sustained Excellence. But you don't master them by scolding and retraining people. These moments are mastered when the workers decide that the moments matter because the workers care, not because the boss is watching them.

That's what focus and reinforcement are about: giving your time and energy to the most important areas and reinforcing them peer to peer, even when the boss isn't around. Let's begin with focus, of which there are two types.

Focus On, Focus In

Many organizations spend a great deal of money attempting to create focus. They write mission statements, lists of values and priorities, and the like. They print these on posters, folders, buttons, and whatnot; encourage everyone in the organization to live up to the mission, values, and/or priorities; and offer inducements to everyone to embrace the new approach as well as consequences for those who do not. This often works at first, but it eventually becomes part of the background noise because it's not precise and directive.

Yes, everyone understands they are to believe in "Going Beyond Precision," "Astonishing Clients with Our Service," "Making Safety #1," or whatever the focus may be. But they don't know what to do about it. How exactly do you go beyond precision? What does "Making Safety #1" really mean? Workers may have been told to stop their machine for a safety issue, but that's a rather vague instruction. What exactly is a safety issue? A machine making a funny noise? Someone seen deviating from a work procedure or rule or taking a critical risk? An alarm going off that others seem to be ignoring? A suspicious individual in the parking lot or approaching the facility entrance?

This is the difference between focusing *on* and focusing *in*.

Focusing *on* directs people's attention to the larger goal, while focusing *in* tells them exactly what to do to achieve that goal. It's the difference between "going beyond precision" and "reject any widget that exceeds tolerance by 0.04% or greater." It's the difference between telling someone to "think ahead" and discussing the details of the work to be accomplished, the associated risks, and controls and precautions that need to be in place or taken.

My firm worked with the AstraZeneca Westborough plant to develop the BEδT Program, which brought two different areas—quality assurance and safety, health, and environment—together to improve both safety and production. Rather than simply encouraging employees to "be safer while producing higher quality stuff," we gave the workers specific things to do. Our goal was to help them focus *on* the larger goal by focusing *in* a small number of very specific behaviors, and to proactively address the many influences on these behaviors.

For example, laboratory workers were given five very clear, simple things to focus *in*:

- Keep your movements slow and deliberate.
- Do not put any body part over an open container, for even the tiniest flake of skin or other item falling from your hand can spoil the batch.

- Always spray your gloves, even after touching a phone or using a tool, and always allow your glove to air-dry rather than rubbing it.
- If you drop something on the floor, let it stay there; don't pick it up and risk contaminating your glove.
- Keep talking to a minimum.

This focusing *in* had a tremendous impact on the site's performance, reducing accidents with injury by fifty percent and contributing to a seventeen-point rise in pristine batches, a measure of quality right first time. In recognition of these achievements, AstraZeneca awarded the Westborough site the Chief Executive's SH&E Award.

We all saw a large-scale example of focusing *in* during the COVID-19 shutdowns, when the government told everyone to wear masks, wash their hands frequently, remain six feet apart from each other, stay at home as much as possible, and isolate if ill. I know this remains a contentious issue, but it is a good example of focusing *in* rather than focusing *on* by instructing us to "stay healthy."

Also notice, in both the AstraZeneca and COVID-19 examples, that the emphasis was on performance. It was on behaviors, not the results. AstraZeneca didn't say that the workers should improve quality and safety. That's the result they wanted, but they focused *in* to encourage certain behaviors: moving slowly and deliberately, not putting body parts over open containers, and so on. Similarly, with COVID-19, the emphasis was on specific behaviors such as frequently washing your hands for at least twenty seconds rather than on the desired result of keeping your hands virus free.

You get the best outcomes by emphasizing and facilitating the desired behavior, the performance, not the results. Our goal may be to improve customer satisfaction by sixty-seven percent, but to truly move the needle we must focus *in*, we must find the few, specific behaviors that, when focused *in*, will produce large effects—often large enough to spill over into other areas and improve many metrics at one.

Which Comes First, On or In?

The ultimate goal is to get your organization's people to focus *in*, but you can't always jump right to *in*. Sometimes, you must begin with *on*. Not too long ago, my wife and I were taking a little boat ride down a river in a third-world country. As we passed by an area where they were building housing, I could see that they were digging deep into the ground without trenching. This raised the risk that the hole would collapse and the workers would be buried. There were other glaringly obvious safety issues, such as using freshly cut, small-diameter trees, with knots, bends, and all, to support second stories and roofs as the concrete was poured and dried.

This construction company has low maturity with respect to safety. In this case, we would have to begin by focusing *on*, getting leadership, management, and workers to embrace the idea that workers' safety is important, that it should be a priority and a value. Before that happens, it would be a waste of time to explain the importance of using the right type of engineered equipment to secure the load of the floors above.

Low-maturity organizations, facilities, shifts, or teams may have to go through a period of focusing *on* before focusing *in*. With high-maturity organizations, such as military special forces and all-star sports teams, you can often jump right to focusing *in*.

Where Should the Focus Be Placed?

What should an organization focus *on* or *in* to become great at what they do? There is no easy answer to that, for every organization is different. Even within an organization, there are differences between shifts, departments, teams, and other areas, and various pieces of the whole have different opportunities and face different challenges.

It may be that one focus works for your entire organization, or perhaps you need different approaches for different pieces of the whole within the framework of the larger organizational focus. I worked with one organization that opened operations in an underdeveloped country. This company required employees to wear safety shoes to work. Since wearing shoes was not typical in nearby villages where the workers lived, the company provided the shoes to the workers. They were grateful for this gift and promptly returned to their villages and sold them for extra money. Now the company is focusing on providing socks to the workforce, for if you don't habitually wear shoes you don't wear socks either, and the workers were suffering from foot blisters.

Deciding where your organization should put its focus, whether *on* or *in* or both, is a matter of great importance for leadership, for you'll be pouring a lot of resources into the focus. Thus, it pays to look for the few items that make the biggest difference. For Safelite, it was switching from an operations focus to a customer focus. For a manufacturer struggling with a high defect rate, it may be finding the few things that will make the most impact on defect rate and focusing *in* those. Yes, there may be ten or fifteen reasons for the high defect rate, but if your research and discussion with the workers finds that two things will have the greatest impact, focus *in* those two. Develop no more than four or five behaviors for each for a maximum of ten new behaviors workers must master over a period of time. That's much more likely to produce positive results than asking workers to deal with all ten or fifteen issues and memorize fifty or a hundred new behaviors.

And when going through your decision-making process, remember this: if you want the workers to take the focus to heart, include them in the decision-making process. You needn't implement all their ideas, but they must feel as if their voice has been heard, as if their ideas have been put into the decision-making algorithm.

Also remember, you're going to be asking your people to welcome these new priorities, values, and behaviors into their heads and hearts. The best way to ensure this happens is to make them feel that the idea is to a certain extent theirs. It won't be entirely theirs, of course, for they don't have the overview of the entire organization—its goals, capabilities, challenges, and resources—that you do. But the more they feel that you've listened to their concerns and have done your best to incorporate their input, the more likely they are to open their heads and hearts.

Six Pennies in the Pocket

It takes a while to learn a new behavior and make it a habit, especially when it isn't your idea to begin with. Even the most dedicated employees need time to adopt new programs and master new behaviors. The less dedicated need more time, and those who aren't on board with the new program will take even more effort.

That's where the Reinforcement Strut on the Bridge comes in. For our purposes, reinforcement means noticing what an individual is doing and responding to it quickly and clearly in either a positive or corrective manner. Reinforcement is much like enforcement, which we talked about in chapter five. But while enforcement is concerned with ensuring compliance and can be treated as a negative, reinforcement leans heavily toward the positive, toward acknowledging people for doing the right thing and thereby cementing the desired behavior(s) in their minds and habits.

Few people get tired of being praised at work, and no one resents being acknowledged by a supervisor or other higher-up, which is why reinforcement can be so powerful. And it need not be complex. Reinforcement may be a simple matter of saying, "I noticed you greeted and thanked that customer. Good job!" Or it may be more complex, with a series of actions leading to a bonus or a free trip.

Of course, for reinforcement to be effective, management and leadership must apply it constantly and consistently. I learned this lesson as a young corporate supervisor at the engineering and construction firm Fluor Daniel. I knew that I was supposed to recognize and praise my people when they did something well, mastered something new, or went above and beyond. I knew that, but I was busy with supervisory stuff and thought that I came off as being insincere, so I didn't give much thought to my reinforcing duties.

My mentor noticed this and told me to put six pennies in my left pocket every morning—this was back in the days when we carried change around. He told me that every time I gave someone specific and sincere recognition for what they're doing well, that is, every time I reinforced good behavior, I was to move one penny from my left to my right pocket. My goal was to move all the pennies from one pocket to the other by the end of day. Wow! That was quite a lesson in how difficult it can be to learn something new. It was especially difficult because I wasn't quite comfortable with the task, and it wasn't my idea to begin with. Many days, I went home with six pennies in the original pocket, and not because I wasn't seeing good stuff happening with the crew. It's because it can be hard to learn and adopt something new! I finally put my mind to my reinforcing duties, and not only did I get better at it, my people got better at what they did too.

Acknowledging people when they do the right thing is a great way to make them want to do it again. And even when you must point out that they're doing it the wrong way, work to understand why, and then help them to understand that you want them to do it the right for their benefit and for everyone's benefit.

Leaders Must Lead for the Followers to Follow

If everything is done properly, that is, if leadership does the following, there's an excellent chance the focus will succeed, both *on* and *in*:

- Identify the overarching thing workers should focus *on*.
- Get input from the workers.
- Develop specific behaviors and actions the workers should focus *in*.
- Master the moment by getting the workers to buy into the program.
- "Move the pennies" by reinforcing desired behaviors.
- Provide a balance of consequences.
- Keep listening to the workers as the program progresses.

Most people will take the focus to heart and put it firmly into their heads, both as a matter of routine and of great personal urgency because they believe in it. And they will encourage others to follow the program. It will become embedded in your culture and will be "the way we do things around here."

Some years ago, we moved to a house with wooden staircases. One of our kids was three at the time, and we were concerned about her falling on the stairs. Naturally, we put up baby gates, but I knew that my kids were going to be going up and down the stairs in other people's houses. So, I encouraged my three-year-old to focus *in* by holding the handrails when she went up or down the stairs. When I saw her holding the handrail, I'd say "Good job. You're holding onto the handrail."

Guess what happened? She saw me not holding the handrail one time and immediately said, "Handrail!" Soon, I had a three-year-old safety czar telling everyone who came to the house to hold the handrail. To this day, even though my older kids are in college, I occasionally hear one of them telling the younger ones, "Handrail!" I had unintentionally gotten them to focus *in* a behavior that helps them remain safe even when I'm not around.

As soon as we give someone an instruction or a list of items to accomplish, introduce them to the company slogan, or encourage them to smile at customers, we have given them something to pay attention to, to try to accomplish. They'll almost certainly do it as long as the boss is around, or the computer is counting their keystrokes, or the camera is recording their actions.

But what will they focus on because they want to? Because they think doing so is vitally important? Because it matters to them personally? That's the purpose of the Focus and Reinforcement Struts, to build capacity within the culture to change the status quo and improve from within.

Insights from Industry Leaders

I asked leaders from a number of industries—including for-profit, non-profit, and governmental—for their insights into focus and reinforcement.

With respect to focus, I asked, Beyond what you expect of your employees, what is one thing that, if your employees would focus on at their discretion, would improve performance or culture significantly?

Here are some of their answers:

Mark Kehne, plant manager, Cardinal FG

- Our history of continuous improvement has shown that having the comfort level and skill set to effectively coach a teammate and to receive coaching from a teammate is the single most effective attribute in our employees that leads to improved performance in all areas.

Kelvin E. Roth, vice president, environmental, health, safety, and quality, CF Industries

- I'm not sure that I could give you one thing right now that would last in perpetuity. Focus is the key, so the question is relevant, but it needs to be asked regularly, not just "one and done." I think of this as a sports team being asked what to focus on. Depends! If you're not hitting well, then batting practice should be the focus. If you're not running the bases well, then running and studying the game is your focus. The best teams continue to analyze data to determine when and where to shift their focus.

Tobias Read, founder, AQRA Group

- Let's look at what should the CEO focus on. I've always used average tenure for my company compared to average tenure for the industry as a key performance indicator, if not the primary key performance indicator (KPI). In fact, I'd say that many CEOs have it wrong. They look at the output as the primary measure—namely, short-term profit. If you can hire great people, then have great retention, you can pay staff more (as churn cost is lower), and they will make profits soar. I genuinely believe CEOs should focus a huge amount of their time on making their company a great place to work so that people stay.

Chris Boleman, president and chief executive officer, Houston Livestock Show and Rodeo

- Focus on the positive. I reiterate this all the time. Be purposeful about it. It is easy to find problems. The reality is it is also easy to find the positives. We just choose not to. To be clear, this doesn't mean you don't handle problems. There are always problems. As humans, we are genetically engineered to fix problems. It is what we do as problem solvers. That is easy. However, it is up to us to make time and take time to find the positives.

- I love it when an experienced, well-respected employee checks on another employee, unsolicited. That's when the cream rises to the top.

Najya Al Hinai, continuous improvement lead, MSEML

- Effective leadership at all levels within the organization. Leaders' behaviors have a ripple effect across the organization, and therefore act as pillars in achieving the organization's success. In today's ever-changing world, leaders need to lead with trust, accountability, and agility in order to encourage growth, remain competitive, move toward digitalization of systems and processes, and manage multi-generational workforces.

Michael Middleton, safety and health director, Georgia Power

- Empathy. We are currently living in unprecedented times, with COVID, monkey-pox, food-shortages, wars, and so forth, and all of these things have a significant impact on the psychological safety of our teammates. As leaders, we have to be empathetic. We have to actively care. We have to show grace to our teammates and show unprecedented leadership during these unprecedented times.

With respect to reinforcement, I asked: What are some examples of how employees reinforce the right things when the boss isn't around?

Here are some of their answers:

Mark Kehne, plant manager, Cardinal FG

- Our employees are trained and encouraged to give feedback to one another when something observed is of concern and especially when something observed is considered a success, such as a "good catch." We also have minor rewards (free soda coupon, an ABCD "Above and Beyond the Call of Duty" award good for a free meal in the cafeteria) that any employee can present to a coworker as positive reinforcement.

Tobias Read, founder, AQRA Group

- In a company with a well-established culture, people believe in the values from within; the cultural value set is not imposed from the top down. In these companies, employees don't change behaviors when the boss is away. They don't take shortcuts. They don't take risks. They do the right things because they want to and they believe in it.

- If employees don't do the right thing when the boss is not around, then that organization has a serious issue. It means that the culture is not true, the employees are dishonest in their commitment, and leadership does not have respect. It is a company that will end up with serious issues or corporate failures, and individuals won't take responsibility.

- In a well-functioning culture, I would expect any person at any level to firmly address nonconformance of a colleague. And if that non-conformance was not accidental or was not willingly remedied by the perpetrator, I'd expect the employee to raise this immediately with somebody with authority, in the knowledge that it would not be tolerated by the company and that there would be no comeback on them.

Jared Matthias, vice president of executive accounts, ChampionX

- My recent realization (last few years) is that this isn't a process-driven or compliance-driven principle. Processes and compliance provide the employee the road map and guard rails to enable them to do the right thing. If they don't want to do the right thing, neither processes nor compliance will drive them to do the right thing. But a culture created around your organization's expectations and an understanding of the end point will improve that success rate (doing the right things). Culture starts with the heart and mind. Do you believe in it and are you proud of it, whatever *it* is?

Kirk Bagnal, owner, Ethostory

- There are a pair of terms in organizational leadership called "cascading information" and "fractal communication." Both of these phrases essentially mean that, regardless of the level within an organization (a company, for example), the message remains the same. It may be phrased a bit differently, or it may be provided from a different angle, but at its core, the message remains the same. As a mid-level leader in an organization, there is nothing more compelling and justifying than when your boss or the company president speaks directly with your department and your team gets to hear exactly what you've been saying—but from the president's perspective. This is cascaded communication, which elicits extreme confidence from front-line workers. When you consider this from the executive leadership perspective, it works the same way. When you (for example), as the senior vice president of operations, meet with frontline manufacturing workers and they can articulate to you the core of the message you have been delivering from "the top" for quite some time, you have confidence that your message is cascading properly, and no matter what fractal lens they see or hear it through, the message is resounding and clear, through and through. This never happens by accident, by the way. I have found that, as leaders, we are called to remind our people more than teach them. In other words, when you feel like you've said something a thousand times and wonder if you should say it again, say it again and again and again. A true test of your leadership communication efficacy is when the people two levels down in your organization can quote you and possibly even imitate your common phrases (with your tone of voice). Imitation (in this case) isn't just a nice form of flattery; it's a confidence-confirming, communication-crowning moment. Build the message, state it, repeat it, ask if it's being understood, state it again, print it, email it, share it widely, and begin again. Remember to KISS and MISS (keep it simple, stupid and make it simpler still).

Joel Simon, partner, Fernelius and Simon

- I ask all employees to be mutually accountable and to work collaboratively. If there is only one person, that is, the boss, who has to keep everything on track, then success can rise or fall based on that one person. Having a sense of shared responsibility and accountability ensures that everyone will be rowing in the same direction, even if the boss is not around.

Mike Diezi, executive director, Spec's Wine, Spirits & Finer Foods

- We may not see the associate actually perform the task, but we see the effects of their outstanding behavior. The holiday season can get very busy for us. Even with a fully staffed location, a very busy store may need a little extra help. One of the indicators of a busy store during a rush is the amount of shopping carts in the parking lot. When a store is busy, the focus is on customer service inside of the store. But without carts available for our guests, we run the risk of not providing the very best experience possible. During the holiday rush I stopped at one of our extremely busy Spec's locations and noticed no carts in the lot. On the way in I ran into one of our associates who had just finished her shift. With a little examination I found out that she had punched out and was on her way home from a very exhausting day. She noticed the assortment of carts in the lot. Instead of heading home, she gave a few more minutes of her time to collect the carts and bring them back inside. This seemed like a small thing, but this was actually very important to the store and to the guests inside.

Najya Al Hinai, continuous improvement lead, MSEML

- A few years back, I visited a few offshore rig sites, and one particular rig had employees who went above and beyond their roles and had created a positive and safe work environment. When I had asked why they did what they did, they responded that their company took care of them. They felt like their leadership genuinely cared for their welfare and wellbeing, said they had a sense of loyalty toward the company, and therefore wanted to show their appreciation through their work. This has always stayed with me, and I try to apply it as best I can in my role.

Michael Middleton, safety and health director, Georgia Power

- When employees are reinforcing those positive fundamental practices in your organization when leadership is not present, your culture is evolving to a place of excellence. So, keep pushing! I strongly advise that you recognize, reinforce, and reward those high-character contributors, as they help maintain a healthy rhythm for the culture of your organization. Quickly celebrate, because, as a mentor always told me, "You can never stop working on safety!" So, immediately challenge these contributors to identify what the next threats and risks are, and figure out how you will empower your employees to mitigate them.

Key Points about Focus and Reinforcement

- Focus and reinforcement are about giving your time and energy to the most important areas and reinforcing them, peer to peer, even when the boss isn't around.
- It pays to look for the few items that make the biggest difference.

- If you want workers to take the focus to heart, include them in the decision-making process.
- Reinforcement means noticing what an individual is doing and responding to it, quickly and clearly, in either a positive or corrective manner.
- Focus and reinforcement build capacity within the culture to change the status quo and improve from within.

Questions to Consider

- What should you focus your people on?
- Where should you develop a focus in?
- On a scale of one to ten, with one indicating you have yet to begin and ten that you are great, how would you rate the effectiveness of the focus element of your organization's Bridge?
- On the same scale of one to ten, what score would you give for the confidence that the right things are being reinforced within your organization's culture?

Chapter Eight – Leadership

Everyone in the organization plays a role in building and maintaining the Bridge to Excellence, no matter what their position on the organizational chart and no matter whether they were present from founding, have only just joined, or are somewhere in between. Every member of the organization contributes to the Bridge in one way or another and, ideally, every member of the organization has a strong sense of ownership in the Bridge.

But there can be only one boss of the Bridge, and that is the leader, whether that organization is a large corporation, navy ship, small NGO, ballet company, or something else. Even if the leader chooses to share responsibility with their leadership team, they are still in charge; they remain the ultimate visionary and decision maker.

It's the leader who guides the organization's activities *vis a vis* the Bridge. The leader *must* do so, otherwise the Bridge will take on a life of its own. It will be nudged, pinched, tugged, and otherwise reshaped by the daily actions within the organization and by the ongoing actions of outside forces. And since changes to the Bridge cannot help but change the organization, the leader who fails to take command of the Bridge also fails to take command of the organization.

Think of your Bridge to Excellence as being a huge topiary made up of numerous bushes and vines that take the shape of a bridge. It stretches from one end of your backyard to the other and climbs high into the sky. You spent months planning it out, selecting just the right combination of plants, and creating unique mixes of fertilizers and soil amendments to nourish and support each element of the Bridge. You've hand-watered your living Bridge daily and carefully intertwined all the shoots and branches, blossoms and stems. You've protected it from the extremes of wind and rain and trimmed it with scientific precision every single day. Guided by your skillful hand, it has grown to be a perfect representation of your organizational Bridge to Excellence.

It's beautiful and precise because you've paid close attention to it. If you were to suddenly stop paying attention, it will continue growing on its own so long as the sun shines and the rain falls. But within a few weeks you'll notice that some of the bushes and vines are growing more aggressively than others, spreading beyond their bounds, and giving strange twists to your Bridge. Without regular application of your special blends of fertilizers and soil amendments, some leaves are turning brown and certain flowers aren't blossoming. One of the larger bushes making up the bridge's foundation is weakening, giving the Bridge a bit of a tilt. Meanwhile, birds are setting up nests in the upper reaches of your Bridge, while bark-eating bugs are munching away at the bottom. Winter comes, and one of the bushes dies of frost; summer comes, and a few vines wither away.

Eventually, your Bridge is no longer yours. It's grown in its own way, reshaped by internal factors, such as some vines and bushes being more enthusiastic growers than others, and external factors, such as weather and animals. The Bridge no longer takes you precisely where you want it to, and wherever it *is* taking you, the journey is no longer smooth.

The same thing will happen with your organization's Bridge if you stop paying attention to it. Your leadership is essential. But what does leadership mean with respect to the Bridge to Excellence?

Leadership is a Mindset

The theory and practice of leadership has evolved over the past many decades, moving from command and control to more of a cooperative, inspirational model. "Cooperative" doesn't mean that leaders must submit issues to a group vote any more than "inspirational" means they should stand in front of the troops, waving the flag and urging them to action. Leaders must still serve as the organization's visionary and pilot. They must make decisions, even the hard ones that result in layoffs and closures. They must do all that leaders in any situation are required to do, but if they want to bring their organization across the Bridge to Excellence they must lead with a mindset of excellence. Not a program of excellence, not a checklist or a series of algorithmic metrics, but a mindset.

Programs, checklists, and metrics are external, and like everything external, are easy to discard when things get tough. But mindset is internal; it becomes not just what you desire but what you are. Excellence becomes a way of thinking, being, and behaving with respect to the Bridge, the organization, and the people making up the organization.

The leader with a mindset of excellence will:

- realize that sustained and repeated results are important,
- work to understand what is driving the results,
- build capacity in the systems to reduce the chances for deviations from expected outcomes,
- recognize that further improvement will always be possible, and it is their responsibility to make that happen,
- grow more and better leaders throughout their company, whether or not these leaders hold a people-leader title,
- work to create a sense of ownership in other developing leaders throughout the company, and
- own everything that happens in the organization, especially the unwanted events and results.

Questions and the Key Question

The leader with a mindset of excellence will have a special relationship to the Bridge. They will feel, in a sense, as if they are the rivets and welds holding the Bridge together. Or perhaps they feel as if they are the lights that shine on and from the Bridge, making it possible for people to cross smoothly and safely. Or maybe they think they are the tour guide, walking people across the Bridge while explaining the parts that are of interest to them. However they think of it, the leader with the mindset of excellence will feel as if they have a powerful link to and affinity for the Bridge. It's their baby, so to speak, and they are determined to ensure that it flourishes.

They will continually consider questions such as these:

- Have I created clear, compelling, and achievable goals as well as a vision for the organization?
- Have I involved others in crafting this vision?
- Have I created one common culture, or are there subcultures within my organization? If so, what are these subcultures, how are they influencing individuals in the organization, and how are they impacting operations?
- Am I developing strong communication signals? Is the information getting where it needs to go and at the right time?
- Am I developing trust? Do I do everything I say that I'm going to do? Am I removing people who destroy trust from the organization, or am I letting them slide by?
- Am I constantly inspecting to make sure things aren't going in the wrong direction? Is excellence my permanent mindset, or do I only think about it on a monthly or quarterly basis?
- What would happen to our Bridge to Excellence if I stopped paying attention for a while?
- And perhaps most importantly of all, am I ensuring that the right things are being reinforced when I'm not around? That is, are my people behaving in the desired manner when I'm not watching them?

In the final year of the American Civil War, Union General Ulysses Grant and Confederate General Robert E. Lee were locked in a no-holds-barred series of battles that raged for six weeks from northern Virginia south toward

Richmond, the Confederate capital. Everyone understood that this bloody fight could determine the war's outcome. Grant pushed forward relentlessly for he knew that if he held back for even a moment, the wily Lee might slip out of his grasp and execute another of the speedy, surprising maneuvers that had befuddled all of Lee's opponents before Grant. In fact, President Abraham Lincoln sent a letter to Grant, urging the general to "hold on with a bull-dog gripe [sic], and chew & choke, as much as possible."[18] Grant did so, hammering and maneuvering his way around Lee to the gates of Petersburg. If Grant could capture the city of Petersburg, the railway lines to nearby Richmond would be cut and the Confederate capital would fall into his hands without a fight.

All through the long and difficult campaign, Grant urged his subordinate commanders to be aggressive and relentless, to hold onto Lee's army with a bull-dog grip. But when Grant sent subordinates ahead to capture the weakly defended Petersburg, they hesitated. Their failure to push ahead relentlessly gave Lee time to reinforce Petersburg and bring Grant's offensive to an abrupt halt. Grant was forced to dig in and besiege Petersburg, losing almost ten months doing so.

General Grant, who had only recently taken command of the Union army, was unable to get all his subordinates to adopt his leadership attitude, his vision for success.

---

[18] Elizabeth D. Samet, "7 Reasons Ulysses S. Grant was One of America's Most Brilliant Military Leaders," History.com, May 13, 2020, https://www.history.com/news/ulysses-s-grant-civil-war-general-strengths.

When he wasn't personally present, making sure everyone followed the plan, they went back to their old ways.

That's why it is vital for the leader to ask themself, "What would happen if I stopped paying attention?" I once worked with a large conglomerate that had a chemical plant in California, a small facility with some fifty employees. The plant manager had five direct reports, and he met with them regularly to read a certain book on leadership. What the book was is not as important as the fact that it represented the manager's leadership philosophy. It was apparently a good philosophy, for the plant ran well.

Once a month, they gathered as a team to read and discuss a chapter. They asked each other, What did we learn from this chapter? How are we going to apply the ideas to what we do? Occasionally, when it was relevant, they'd discuss how to apply the ideas to their lives outside of work.

Sometime later, the plant Manager was promoted within the organization and left the factory. Time passed while the company was deciding who the new manager would be, and they noticed that things were going quite well without anyone in that slot. The plant seemed to be running itself because the former manager had imbued his subordinates with his leadership philosophy. Although he was not present, they were behaving as if he was. The former manager's Bridge continued to flourish even though he wasn't there anymore. The plant performed nicely without a manager for a couple of years, until the parent organization decided that they should appoint a new manager for business reasons. The values that the original manager instilled continue to this day, and this factory continues to be the top performer in all operating categories within the larger business.

This leader, this manager, discovered what would happen when he was not there to watch. And I'm sure that he was pleased with what he saw.

A Brief Word on Un-Excellence

There are leaders who don't care about organizational excellence because they are perfectly happy being average or even subpar. I say this without criticism, for there are situations in which being average or less is just fine or impossible to rise above.

If, for example, you're the sole supplier of a certain item and people have no choice but to buy from you, you may not care about being excellent. If you're in a low-margin business with fierce competition, you probably can't afford to pay the higher wages necessary to attract top-flight talent and take other steps that lead to excellence. If your organization has high turnover, you may be forced to focus on training and compliance, with no time or resources left over to shoot for excellence. Perhaps you're a franchise operator so tightly bound by the organization's rules, requirements, and restrictions that you have little opportunity to rise above. Or maybe you're making enough money being so-so and see no reason to change.

It may be that you don't want to, don't need to, or can't have a state-of-the-art Bridge to Excellence. Perhaps a rope bridge is all you want or can have. If that takes you to where you want to be, it's sufficient.

Spreading the Mindset

However, if you dream of being excellent, you must adopt the mindset of excellence and then spread it throughout the organization. Spread it to the point that everyone voluntarily goes above and beyond, even when the boss is not looking; even when there is no reward for doing so other than the satisfaction of being excellent; even to the point that they become leaders, coaching and urging others to be excellent. Imbuing everyone in your organization with a sense of leadership, tied to your goals, is the highest level of leadership that you can achieve.

Some time ago, a mining company was acquired, and an executive of the acquired company took the bosses of the purchasing company on a tour. This mine had long ago set up all the standard safety precautions, but the harsh reality is that you can't guard against all the risks in some environments. In this operation there was a huge conveyor belt, almost a mile long. It was so long that it was impossible to put up guards all along its length. Since they couldn't have physical barriers that would prevent people from falling into, leaping over, or otherwise interacting with the belt in an inappropriate manner, the company created a cultural expectation that "you never break the plane."

Think of a football field, which has end zones on either end and a playing field in between. There's a plane between the field and the end zone, an invisible wall, with no thickness whatsoever. As soon as a runner carrying the football breaks the plane, that is, crosses from the field into the end zone, they score a touchdown.

Leadership had created a similar plane in this mining operation: an imaginary, invisible wall that ran along the length of the conveyor belt, from the beginning to the end. They created a rule that said the plane cannot be broken and got the workers to absorb the rule into the culture. At this point, it was more than a rule: it was a "way we do things around here" that really mattered to everyone. It mattered because they understood the *why* behind the *way*: Breaking the plane could lead to serious injury, so we don't want to break it. And we don't want to see others break it either.

During the tour with the new owners, the executive from the mining operation showed the new bosses what they had purchased. At some point the executive stopped to explain something. He happened to be standing right next to the conveyor belt, and he happened to talk with his hands. A janitor sweeping up nearby saw that this guy, whom he did not know, was breaking the plane. It was only with his hands, for he clearly had no intention of jumping on the belt or doing something else foolish. Nevertheless, he was breaking the plane.

So, the janitor went over, tapped the guy on the shoulder and said, "Excuse me, sir. You're breaking the plane. That's very unsafe, so can you please not do that?" This janitor didn't know he was speaking to a high-level executive and the new owners. Nor did he care who they were. His attitude was, "This is my site, and I take ownership of it. I'm not going to let you do something that's going to put yourself at risk. I don't care who you are; I'm going to say something."

Surprised, the executive stopped breaking the plane and thanked the janitor for helping him avoid an injury. After the tour, the executive found the local manager and told him what had happened, adding that the janitor had done exactly the right thing, and he hoped more employees would do the same.

The head of this mining operation had hit the leadership jackpot by adopting a successful philosophy, building a great Bridge, and inspiring the people in the organization to take ownership of the Bridge and become leaders on their own—even if they didn't have an official leadership position.

I saw a powerful example of official leadership spreading the mindset when I went to assess a plant outside of Indianapolis. This plant, which was part of a larger organization, had the best scores in all areas of business results and culture. And surveys showed that the workers at this plant firmly believed that leadership supported safety and other things of concern to the workers. The corporate team and I went there to figure out what was going so very right in order to share what we learned with other locations.

I interviewed a great many employees at the plant, and about a third of them told the same story, which happened sometime in the past. One day, a worker saw three visitors come into his area. One of the three was wearing the required eye protection, but the other two were not. So, this man, at his discretion, stopped what he was doing, approached the visitors and said something to the effect of, "Safety is really important around here. If you wouldn't mind coming with me, there's a bin of glasses on the wall over there. We'll get you some glasses." He walked them to the bin, helped them select safety glasses, wished them a good visit, and returned to his work.

This employee didn't realize that Jennifer, the Assistant Plant Manager, was nearby talking with someone and witnessed this exchange. Jennifer went up to man, shook his hand and said, "Thank you very much for what I saw you do. Safety is really important to me, and I'm glad it's important to you to help our visitors be safe."

Now interestingly, around that time other employees had been saying things like, "Production is king around here," and "They only care about production." But now this employee could say, "I don't think that's true." The story of the manager thanking a worker for attending to safety quickly went viral.

When I gave that feedback to Jennifer during my visit, she had no memory of the event. For her, it was a routine exchange, thanking an employee for attending to safety. Yet it was important enough to the workers that it shaped and changed the storytelling in the organization, and over time it changed the level of discretionary effort and helped change the culture. The workers learned that leadership would take the time to reward the behavior it wanted to see, so people did more of it.

Going from "Paycheckers" to Leaders

Often, when working with organizational leaders, I tell them about the Employee Effort Scale of one to ten, where one is barely showing up for work on time, five is doing just what is necessary to collect a paycheck, and ten is consistently going above and beyond. I ask them to give me the average number for their organization. Usually, the answer is five or six. Then I ask what level on that same scale is necessary just to collect a paycheck. Invariably, the answer is five or six. In other words, in far too many organizations, far too many people operate at the "paycheck collection level."

If your organization is at this level, it will be average. Certain nooks and crannies of the organization may be performing well, perhaps because key people in the right positions are driving those areas. But overall, you will struggle, for your "paycheckers" have no interest in excellence.

How do you go from being an organization bogged down by paycheckers to one flush with people eager to push for excellence? How do you move the fives up to six or seven, and the sixes and sevens up to nine and ten? There are no universal techniques for doing so, for each organization faces its own challenges, and these challenges evolve over time. However, I can say that the process begins with the leader asking himself a series of questions:

- Am I creating crystal-clear clarity around the rules?
- Do I ensure that the rules are enforced fairly and firmly?
- Do I excite people about our culture and help them get focused in?
- Do I make it clear to my people that I care about them?
- Am I developing teamwork?
- Am I confident that people are striving for excellence when I'm not around to watch?
- Do my actions and behaviors encourage discretionary action?

In short, am I, the leader, investing in excellence, selecting people for excellence, training for excellence, demanding excellence, and then continuously monitoring for that excellence? Have I operationalized excellence? Have I created an enticing vision of excellence, made it part of the organization's lifeblood? Have I explained to everyone what excellence is and gotten them to adopt the mindset of excellence on their own? Have I turned them into leaders—all of them, no matter what their position or responsibilities? Do they encourage others to be excellent?

It would be unrealistic to expect a leader to create an organization composed entirely of workers scoring nines and tens on the scale. But every time you successfully encourage your people to add in more discretionary effort—and help them do so by removing barriers to that effort—you make your Bridge more robust. When workers are enthusiastic about the company mission, the organizational culture automatically improves. When they have a clear understanding of their objectives and expectations, focus sharpens. When values are shared across the organization, teamwork improves. When people feel they can use their strengths at work every day, discretionary effort improves. When they feel as if their excellent work will be recognized, trust between leadership and workers rises.

Perpetual Excellence

In the Middle Ages, crafty inventors struggled to develop a perpetual motion machine, a device that, once built and set in motion, would continue to run on its own without any additional energy inputs. Unfortunately, such a device violates the laws of thermodynamics and is quite literally impossible.

But perhaps great leaders can create perpetual motion within their organizations by relentlessly pursuing excellence. The motion of the organization becomes perpetual because you, the leader, infuse and inspire others in the organization, and when you are flagging, you are infused and inspired by the amazing things your people do entirely on their own. Everyone feeds off the excellence of each other, and your pursuit of sustained excellence becomes natural and effortless.

Insights from Industry Leaders

I asked leaders from a number of industries— including for-profit, non-profit, and governmental—for their insights into leadership. Specifically, I asked: What does outstanding leadership look like to you within your company?

Here are some of their answers:

Tobias Read, founder, AQRA Group

- Set a very clear and compelling goal that is relevant, exciting, and achievable.
- Communicate to staff regularly and honestly at different levels. Keep people informed, answer questions honestly, and treat people like adults.
- Care for your people. However hard it may be, visit every office, every plant, every department. Be present and get to know your people. Listen to them, listen to their ideas, and give personal feedback.
- Be honest, be fair, and have integrity.

Kelvin E. Roth, vice president, environmental, health, safety, and quality, CF Industries

> Leadership means you have a strategy and goal and then help people move toward that goal. That doesn't come in one style or package.

Marc Gilbertson, vice president and facility general manager, East Dubuque Nitrogen Fertilizers

- I am a firm believer in servant leadership. I think it's hard to ask employees to care about what they are doing if you don't care about them or the things that make their jobs difficult. The single best way, in my opinion, to show an employee that you care is to help solve problems that they care about, big or small, impactful or insignificant. I'm thinking about writing a book; the title will be "Just Fix the

Pigeon Problem!" It's based on a recent experience I had with an operator who brought to my attention a problem with pigeons in his area. I asked if he had mentioned this to others and of course he had, without success. I think to myself, what a perfect opportunity to show this guy you care—and it only takes a phone call or two.

Chris Boleman, president and chief executive officer, Houston Livestock Show and Rodeo

- The value of learning, that is the key. Knowing that every single one of us has a line, and on one side of the line is everything we know. The other side of the line is everything we don't know. To me, outstanding leadership is getting everyone to be willing to push that line into the area of the unknown. Is it uncomfortable? Hell yes, but it is *the* way for the organization to grow, adapt, and continue to be successful.

Ed Senavaitis, director of corporate safety, Buckeye Partners, LP

- A selfless, titleless, humble, and helpful coach and mentor

Kirk Bagnal, owner, Ethostory

- Leadership is about inviting the people that you are responsible for into a beautiful and compelling story where they get to be the hero.

Mike Diezi, executive director, Spec's Wine, Spirits & Finer Foods

- With all skills, one must start at the beginning to build the foundation. Of all the people to lead, the toughest person to lead is oneself. I think that is because it is sometimes difficult to evaluate ourselves to find our deficiencies and growth opportunities. Self-motivation can also be a challenge.

- That said, the first indicator I look for in a leader, or budding leader, is how well they handle their own business. Are they on time? Are they in the proper attire for their task? Are they prepared? Do they require additional motivation, or can they self-start? Notice, motivation is *not* the same as direction or training. A leader can ask for direction or clarity. The important distinction is that asking questions is continuous learning and growth, which we encourage.

- Secondly, we expand on the "give a dang" factor. Attitude is critically important. People are inspired by those with a positive energy. If a group is led by an individual with a hostile attitude, they work under coercive conditions. They will not like their jobs, and those who are most marketable (the most valuable to the company) will go elsewhere. Those that do stay will not be as productive or successful in their endeavor. I have also noticed, in my experience, that a team that works under these conditions will work when the supervisor is around and tend to ease off when not being driven by the forceable overseer. Also notice that my term for this coercive individual is "leader." While this is a style, I do not consider this a quality of a true leader. A positive leader who appreciates those in their care will inspire. When the crew is inspired, they set themselves to their tasks with a positive, productive attitude.

- Finally, I believe that communication has been a big part of my most successful leadership tenures. While a large portion of the communication is in the direction and training from the leader to the team, it is important for the leader to welcome communication in the other direction as well. A dialogue is greater than a monologue, and a good leader will welcome feedback. When a leader properly trains those in their care, the team will eventually, and should by design, attain knowledge that surpasses the capacity of the leader. It is in the leader's best interest to be open to the team.

Commander Richard H. Tetrev, US Navy (retired)

- Decide, delegate, and disappear. Basically, give them the training to do the job, test them on their ability to perform the task, and when they have passed, give them the assignment and get out of the way.

Mark Kehne, plant manager, Cardinal FG

- Our organization is a goals-and-expectations-focused team, with coaching as the tool to achieve those goals. Outstanding leadership has clearly defined and communicated goals and expectations, focuses on what is within one's own realm of control, coaches team members to achieve continuous improvement toward those goals, and holds oneself and the team members accountable for the results. Accountability includes both what is done when the goal is not met as well as what is done when the goal is met or exceeded.

Joseph McBrearty, chief executive officer, Canadian Nuclear Laboratories

- For over forty years I have been involved in the operation, maintenance, refurbishment, and decommissioning of nuclear facilities and also the training, qualification, and leadership of nuclear industry operators and leaders. I will not say that I have seen it all; thankfully, I have not. But I have seen enough to believe to I can offer some thoughts or lessons learned throughout these years.

I want to start out with a story, initially seen through the eyes of a fourteen-year-old boy. My father was responsible for the maintenance of the infrastructure of a large percentage of Baltimore County, Maryland public schools, and on occasion he would take me into the boiler rooms of these facilities when he went to do or oversee maintenance or operations. (There would probably be something illegal about that today, but I think the statute of limitations has expired!) Here was my sense and what I saw: I saw high pressure and high temperature hazardous systems being worked on without a lot of formality. (I would not grasp that until much, much later.) And all of the noise, alarms, steam, and fire from the boilers and high electrical energy terrified me but not my dad.

I told myself I would never work in a job that would expose me to anything like that. So, fast forward to nine years later, as I leaned up against a massive, very high temperature and high pressure steam pipe, across the aisle from an abundance of high-pressure air and hydraulic systems and high voltage electrical systems, just a few feet away from an operating high power nuclear reactor, several hundred feet underwater, I felt completely safe and right at home!!

How could that be? How could a fourteen-year-old kid who was scared of all of those things come to embrace the technology and the inherent risks? Well, certainly years of training in the US Navy's Nuclear Propulsion Program (NNPP) went a long way to establish that comfort level. But there was something even more fundamental, and it was based on NNPP principles. I felt safe because I had complete faith and confidence in the design, the construction, the maintenance, and the operation of my ship. And that was due to—and reinforced countless times since then—the standards of training, qualification, excellence, accountability, and responsibility driven into each man on that ship. And it did not matter if they were the most junior enlisted crewman or the captain: the standards and the expectations were all the same. We all relied on each other to get our mission done and to get home safely.

I also know that, like most military organizations, the crew worked together to succeed and help and look out for each other. Camaraderie at its finest.

So, what are the lessons I have learned from the NNPP and subsequent assignments?

Care for your people, first and foremost.

Ensure you plan your ops to the best of your ability, and use lessons learned.

Adjust your plan as conditions change.

Never be overly confident.

Listen to others.

We do dangerous things, and we are often put in harm's way, since that may be our job. But if you get hurt or killed before your mission, you are useless and you are now endangering others (for example, the USS Atlanta's grounding off of Gibraltar and the impact on USAF operations over Libya).

Treat those that you work with as though they are your loved ones. You have been entrusted by your people's families to do the best for their loved ones. Never forget that.

Going to the morgue is something that I do not wish on anyone. Unfortunately, I have not been so lucky as to avoid having to do so.

Talk with someone who has been seriously injured on the job. It is an eye opening and sobering experience.

As a manager or as a leader, your efforts and thoughts about safe operations do not end as you leave the site. You have to be constantly thinking about the what ifs, and do not be afraid to call and ask questions or stop something. I have been the last piece of Swiss cheese several times, and it is not fun.

Reward and empower your folks. Let them know you trust them, but always have their backs. As a senior leader, it is unlikely anyone will have more experience than you.

Throwing your people in the deep end with no knowledge of swimming may sound like a great idea to some, but it is downright stupid.

Our folks and leaders must have pride in where they work, be it in the physical plant or the mission or whatever. Pride drives performance for many folks.

It is the leader's responsibility to insist on hard and effective training. Not all will make it. We have seen too many occasions where we have let training and qualifications lapse or slowly degrade without ensuring standards are met.

Some folks will not cut it. They can be given opportunities, but at the end day, each individual is responsible for their own decisions.

Always drive to the highest standard. That is why I was so comfortable on that first submarine. Admiral Rickover understood it, and lived it, and made his people live it.

You must have hard-hitting, impactful assessments that staff and management respect and frankly are a bit fearful of. Fear of failure can be a great motivator. And remember, each person is driven by different motivations.

Don't get wrapped up in the touchy feely, politically correct way to deal with people. While this may sound harsh, their lives are more important than how they may feel one day.

Leaders and societies must drive resiliency. What we do is hard. How we get there and prep our people is even harder some days, and people will fail. Get over it. The most successful folks have likely failed dozens of times.

Not everyone is going to be a US Navy SEAL; that can be a harsh reality to some. However, our systems must be able to select the right people. We cannot tolerate mediocracy in order to meet quotas or political aspirations. We are in a business that requires the utmost professionalism and trust in one other and in each other's abilities.

Leaders must be able to find and discern the high-potential staff who will likely excel. It is important to note that these folks will come from all walks of life, and many times the ones who are the most visible are not the highest performers. Often the bombastic ones are the least capable and are the most overly confident, without good reason.

Key Points about Leadership

- The leader who wishes to take command of the organization must also take command of the Bridge.
- If you dream of being excellent, you must adopt the mindset of excellence and then spread it throughout the organization.
- Everyone in the organization plays a role in building and maintaining the Bridge to Excellence.
- When people feel they can use their strengths at work every day, discretionary effort improves. When they feel as if their excellent work will be

recognized, trust between leadership and workers improves.

- Imbuing everyone in your organization with a sense of leadership, tied to your goals, is the highest level of leadership that you can achieve.

Questions to Consider

1. What percentage of your leadership are creating an environment where their employees want to contribute more than what is necessary to collect a paycheck?

2. What percentage of your leaders are agents of change, compared to those focused on managing the status quo?

3. Do you have leadership capacity to align cultures within your organization and to align the cultures with the systems to prevent unwanted events?

4. On a scale of one to ten, with one indicating you have yet to begin and ten that you are great, how would you rate confidence in the leadership element of your bridge?

Chapter Nine – Trust

In 1783, General George Washington, commander in chief of the Continental Army, presented himself before the Continental Congress to deliver a speech which concluded with these words: "Having now finished the work assigned me, I retire from the great theatre of action, and bidding an affectionate farewell to this august body, under whose orders I have so long acted, I here offer my commission, and take my leave of all the employments of public life."

This may seem to us today to be an event of minor notice, a general resigning from his position ("offer my commission") at the end of a long war and going home. But it sent shockwaves through the young nation and across the ocean to Europe, setting Washington on the path to becoming the Father of our Nation.

Washington was not the most brilliant of battlefield generals; he's never spoken of in the same breath as Julius Caesar, Napoleon, or Patton. In fact, when the Continental Congress was considering candidates to head the brand new Continental Army, the fact that Washington hailed from Virginia, the largest of the thirteen colonies-turned-states, was just as important a consideration as his prior battlefield experience.

Fortunately, Washington was equal to the task. He proved himself a great leader by holding his ragtag army together through terrible times and inspiring his oft-defeated men to keep trying, once more, and then once more again. Finally, in 1781, with strong support from the French navy and army, he trounced the British at

Yorktown, effectively bringing the war to an end. He remained at his post until the peace treaty between the Americans and the British was signed in 1783, then went to Congress to resign his commission as commander in chief.

This resignation turned Washington into an international sensation. Up until then, it was expected that a triumphant general would take up—or seize—the reins of power of a nation with a weak government, which is what the nation was in 1783. Indeed, some of Washington's subordinates had suggested that he stage a coup, but he refused. Instead, he went home, demonstrating beyond all doubt that he embraced the republican culture of the new nation and was willing to go above and beyond to protect it—which, in this case, meant walking away from his power base and from a throne. When Britain's King George III heard of this, he is said to have remarked, "If [Washington] does that, he will be the greatest man in the world."[19]

Washington certainly became the greatest man in the new nation. From the start, the thirteen states bickered, sometimes seriously so, and often refused to cooperate with each other and with the feeble central government—hardly a promising beginning for a new nation. Floundering, they turned to the idea of a Constitutional Convention to iron out differences and

---

[19] Joseph Hillman, "Resignation of a Military Commission," *Washington Library*, https://www.mountvernon.org/library/digitalhistory/digital-encyclopedia/article/resignation-of-military-commission/.

repair the central government. Some states were doubtful of the idea, but it was the widespread trust in George Washington, who would serve as president of the convention, that made it possible for the gathering to succeed. He wasn't the best candidate to head the convention in terms of education, in which he was deficient compared to other luminaries, or political experience. He was not considered to be an original or deep thinker, nor was he a great writer or speaker. But he was trusted. The Constitutional Convention was only able to devise the structure for the new government because everyone understood that the head of this new government, the very first president of the United States, would be George Washington, the trusted man.

After serving two terms as president, Washington once again walked away from power by announcing he would not serve a third term. He did so to prevent the presidency from becoming a perpetual position, a throne in all but name. This was, like the resignation from his post as commander in chief, a remarkable act at the time.

Many people disagreed with Washington's acts and policies as commander in chief and president, sometimes vehemently so. But he was trusted to keep the larger goal in mind, which is why he was entrusted with key positions at the founding, which is why he is the Father of our Nation.

As Thomas Jefferson said when Washington reluctantly agreed to become president, "We cannot, Sir, do without you."

Trust is increasingly rare in the United States. According to a recent Gallup poll, very few Americans have a "great deal" or "quite a lot" of confidence in the following groups:

- congress – 7%
- television news – 11%
- the criminal justice system – 14%
- big business – 14%
- newspapers – 16%
- the Supreme Court – 25%[20]

And according to the Pew Research Center, only 21% of Americans trust the federal government to do what is right "just about always" or "most of the time."[21]

We live in an era in which trust seems like a quaint relic of the past, and "the other side" is felt to be not just wrong but out to get you. This means that many of your workers are primed to mistrust your organization, its leadership, and the information and training you provide them. Many of them are primed to laugh off your slogans and value statements, and to resist your rules and regulations. How do you get them to trust you? Trust is what's required if they are to go above and beyond for the organization. They must buy in to your organization's

---

[20] "Confidence in Institutions." *Gallup*, https://news.gallup.com/poll/1597/confidence-institutions.aspx.
[21] "Public Trust in Government: 1958–2022." Pew Research Center, Washington DC, June 6, 2022. https://www.pewresearch.org/politics/2022/06/06/public-trust-in-government-1958-2022/.

values, culture, rules, and everything else. And they must buy into you, the leader. They won't do so unless they trust you.

Developing trust requires the following:

- communication, honesty, vulnerability, transparency
- making sure everyone feels as if their voice is being heard
- consistent behavior over time
- others understanding the intent behind your actions; that is, that the *why* behind any changes is clearly understood by those affected by the change
- strong relationships

Let's take a look at some of these trust builders.

Communication Builds Trust

Beginning in 2020, as COVID-19 and public-health restrictions began to spread, more and more companies began using contact-tracking devices, such as a badge worn at work. The badge has a built-in proximity sensor that, among other things, alerts you if you come within a certain distance of someone else with a badge. Before COVID-19, these devices were often used to control access to buildings for security reasons. Once COVID-19 struck, it quickly became a tool to manage virus tracing. If someone notified management that they had COVID-19, they could look back through the computer records to see who they had come in contact with recently and ask those people to stay home and isolate.

This was tremendously helpful because otherwise management would not have known whom they had come in contact with. Erring on the side of caution, they might tell an entire shift or department to remain home, causing tremendous fear and work disruption.

Soon, many more workers were required to wear contact tracing devices. To management, this was a positive because it would protect the workers as well as the organization. But to workers abruptly being told to wear the devices, it was suspicious. "They say it's for Covid," one worker might say to another, "but what are they really going to do? See how long we spend in the bathroom?"

When we become suspicious, we tend to look for things that "prove" our suspicions are correct and to ignore those which show they are not. This is called confirmation bias, and it only takes one event—like being told to wear a "badge that rats me out to management"— to take a big bite out of trust.

That's why it is important to consider trust every time you roll out a new procedure, process, tool, pay scale, schedule, or anything else. It's vital that leadership be transparent in explaining the reasons why to the fullest extent possible.

Buy-in Builds Trust

Leadership communicating with workers is a great beginning, but it's just half of what should be a two-way conversation.

Imagine that the leadership of a large factory decides to replace the machinery. Leadership announces that the new machines will be installed on a certain day, has the operators attend training sessions to learn how to use the new machines ahead of time, and posts additional training videos on the company website. Leadership also has the supervisors talk with the operators, acknowledging that the transition to the new machines will be difficult. The learning curve will be steep, and this will be taken into consideration if workers make mistakes. The supervisors also explain that the new machines are being installed to allow the factory to remain competitive by manufacturing more advanced items.

At first glance, leadership's rollout of the new machines seems wonderful, filled with communication and information. But it's missing something: feedback from the workers.

Leadership talked, but they did not listen. They did not invite the workers to speak to them. They didn't gather together key employees and say, "How is this going to impact you?"

I've seen what can happen when leadership makes decisions without consulting the workers. I've seen, for example, machines with three pinch points be replaced with machines that have seven. (A pinch point is a place on a machine where two parts come together and a hand or other body part can be pinched, cut, or crushed.) Changing to the new machines may have made sense from a financial point of view, but it made the workers' work more dangerous.

168

I've also seen new machines rolled out with great fanfare, only for the workers to discover that certain valves or access points have been placed such that they're nearly impossible to reach without clambering over the machine or twisting yourself into an awkward and possibly dangerous position.

Problems like these arise when decisions are made at the "blunt end of the stick," back at headquarters, rather than at the "sharp end of the stick," where the work is performed. The people back at headquarters can easily overlook these issues because they are far removed not just from the dangers but also from the reality of how work is actually performed, compared to how the work is designed on paper to be performed.

When you're asking people to buy into a decision, it's important to give them the opportunity to weigh in. If not, you're not truly asking for buy-in; you're just briefing them on a decision you've already made, and that's usually not well received. Doing so plays right into confirmation bias and "proves" you don't care about the workers.

I know of organizations which practice comprehensive management of change methodology. Before bringing in new machines or making other changes to the work—especially when making large capital changes—they pull together teams of individuals who actually perform the work. The workers are asked to assess the proposed changes and sign off on them before final approvals.

This is a good example of leadership really communicating with workers about change, not just engaging in a one-way monologue.

What Works for You?

Take a moment to reflect on what has led you to trust a person, process, service, or company?

And over the course of your career, what have you found that builds trust, and what have seen destroy trust? What has worked for you personally, as a leader, to get people to trust you? And have you noticed that knowing your people, really knowing what motivates and demotivates them, and responding appropriately, plays a big role in building trust?

Trust Is Never a Given

Trust is like a bucket of water filling very slowly, a drop at a time. But it only takes a second to kick it over and lose all the trust you've built over the years.

In 1999, the head of the French tire manufacturer Michelin SCA announced that ten percent of the company's European workers would be laid off. With nearly the same breath, he also announced that company profits rose twenty percent.[22] The announcement stunned the French people and severely weakened workers' trust

---

[22] Joseph Fitchett, "With Its Layoffs, Michelin Skids into a Hornet's Nest." *New York Times*, September 15, 1999, https://www.nytimes.com/1999/09/15/news/with-its-layoffs-michelin-skids-into-a-hornets-nest.html.

in the company: "We're making more money, and those jerks are laying us off?!"

Generations of trust between the company and its workers as well as between the company and the public vanished all at once. It took ten years, plus a commitment to continually collaborate with its workers, for Michelin to regain the trust lost.[23]

This story explains why the Trust Truss sits at the top of the Bridge to Excellence, in the center. Every piece of the Bridge is essential. Indeed, without the Compliance Pillar the Bridge could not exist, while without the Culture Pillar it could not reach across the river to Sustained Excellence. Every piece has its place, but it's Trust that sits at the top center.

Weaken or destroy the Trust Truss, and the connection between the Management Pillar and the Workers Pillar is lost. The link between the Leadership and Teamwork cables will be lost as well. The entire top half of the Bridge will be severely weakened, and the whole Bridge will rattle, wobble, and sway in the wind as waves of competition, technological disruption, regulatory changes, and all the rest beat against the Bridge.

Damaging or destroying Trust is like kicking the capstone out of an arch. The Bridge may stand for a while,

---

[23] Lane Lambert, "Good News for Disgraced Companies: You Can Regain Trust." *Working Knowledge*, Harvard Business School, July 07, 2021, https://hbswk.hbs.edu/item/good-news-for-disgraced-companies-you-can-regain-trust.

but it will be fatally weakened and sooner or later will collapse.

Everything in the Bridge builds up to Trust, and from Trust flows the "glue" that holds it all together, the "blood" the nourishes it, the "electrons" that energize it, and the "luminosity" that makes the Bridge a beacon to all—to the members of your organization and to all who look at, look to, and interact with your organization.

Sometimes, trust builds quickly and practically automatically. You'll see this with firefighters, special forces in the military, line workers, and others in high-stress or extreme-risk jobs. Going through tough situations together and overcoming challenges builds strong relationships and creates a strong desire to maintain those relationships. In units such as these, relationships and trust can be built and reinforced quickly.

Of course, not all organizations are in high-pressure, high-risk situations. For them, the challenge is to build a high level of trust, without putting people through harrowing or risky situations. Some organizations attempt to do so by developing and leading exercises that allow teams to accomplish challenging acts. But for this to succeed, you, the leader, must understand your people well and must know what will work best with this unique group of individuals to build trust.

What can you do in your organization to build trust or strengthen the trust you already have?

Insights from Industry Leaders

I asked leaders from a number of industries—including for-profit, non-profit, and governmental—for their insights into trust. Specifically, I asked, Why does trust look like within your company culture?

Here are some of their answers:

Kolin Ibrahim, senior manager, environmental, health, and safety, Hess Corporation

- It is safe for people to speak their mind without fear of negative consequences.

Mark Kehne, plant manager, Cardinal FG

- The foundation of trust is open communication. The visible indicator of trust within the organization is seeing the willingness of team members to ask a peer, a subordinate, or a leader for information or feedback.

Tobias Read, founder, AQRA Group

- Trust is a process which is built up over time, based on four things:
  o making promises and delivering on them
  o always looking out for the best of the company, taking bold decisions, and making the company successful
  o always being seen to be fair and even-handed, perhaps occasionally tough; not being a push-over; not having biases or unwarranted favorites within the team; promoting and praising on merit
  o praising those that deserve credit and never taking credit for the work of others

Todd Nall, president, ShowBox Exhibits

- When we leave a meeting clearly knowing what each other's roles are.

Marc Gilbertson, vice president and facility general manager, East Dubuque Nitrogen Fertilizers

- Hearing consistent messages builds trust, even if the message is not the answer you're looking for. It means being able to professionally voice concerns, no matter how ugly, and being acknowledged, respected, and heard without reprisal.

Chris Boleman, president and chief executive officer, Houston Livestock Show and Rodeo

- A lot of trust, from a leadership standpoint, is "letting go." All leaders go through a process: The first step in the process is one of a hands-on manager. They want to see how everything is done, from beginning to end. They feel a deep need to try and understand and be able to do it. While a little of this is good, the quicker a leader gets out of that, the better. They have to have a firm understanding of the work, to be able to lead, to develop the vision, to think strategically, to see where the world is going, and how that impacts the organization. In doing so, they give up the day-to-day to the appropriate team members. In other words, get out of the way and let people do their jobs. Jump in when needed, provide guidance, stay engaged and up to speed, but let them lead their teams. That is what trust looks like.

Kirk Bagnal, owner, Ethostory

- I had a boss and mentor early in my career in the US Army. Major Jeff Witsken was a very principled, methodical, caring, but demanding leader. I had recently received a promotion and began working for him. The first day I met with him, he informed me that he was an "incrementalist leader." I wasn't exactly sure what that was. In fact, I had no idea. I just hoped it wasn't contagious. He went on to tell me that he would trust me to lead my organization well, but he wanted me to keep him informed of key initiatives that I was working on by doing check-in meetings twice weekly. He told me how this would allow him to re-direct if necessary, or apply pressure, or provide the support I would need to move things along faster. What a gift this turned out to be. Not only would we meet twice a week, but I found our meetings started happening even more frequently and informally. As I established trust with him (and he with me), we then were able to share ideas together, brainstorm, try things out, and move very quickly. He was in no way a micro-manager or a controller. He was a mentor and a very engaged, developmental leader who taught me early in my career how to establish methodical rhythm in leadership to keep things moving forward all the time. So, I have become an "incrementalist leader" as well. I guess it was contagious after all. As a footnote, I was the Battalion Maintenance Officer for a US Army Armored Tank Battalion in the First Infantry Division when I worked for Major Jeff Witsken. That battalion received the Army

Maintenance Excellence Award as the best battalion in all of the US Army. It was a bittersweet moment because the award was given a few months after both Major Witsken and I had left for other duty assignments; however, we knew we had built a foundation that left a legacy that equipped them to be the best prepared they could possibly be to go to war—which they did just a short time later.

Mike Diezi, executive director, Spec's Wine, Spirits & Finer Foods

- We have almost four thousand employees across the state, and we continue to grow and provide more jobs for Texans on a regular basis. They are spread over two hundred locations. It is critical that we know that our associates are going to work to do their best regardless of their position within the company. We have to ensure that each associate understands that their ability to make correct and responsible decisions will help the company which, in turn, helps each and every employee.

- There is no physical way that senior management can be everywhere at all times. The company entrusts its future to its field management to operate the stores properly and responsibly. It entrusts the buyers to purchase carefully and prudently and seriously accept their fiduciary responsibility. We trust our drivers to make efforts to be safe, our cashiers to check identification at the register. At the risk of being repetitive, we are in the people business. All leaders are. If we cannot trust our most valuable asset, our people, we cannot succeed.

Commander Richard H. Tetrev, US Navy (retired)

- A good example of trust is me as a mission commander, a junior officer O3 (Lieutenant in the Navy, Captain in the Army) sent on a detachment, as leader of a crew of twelve, to an island in the Indian Ocean to find submarines or spy ships, thousands of miles away from my home base. My superiors entrusted me with the lives of those twelve crew members and a multimillion-dollar airplane. I am not the only one: in each squadron there were nine to ten aircraft and twelve crews stationed around the world.

Key Points about Trust

- In order to develop trust within your organization, you, the leader, must understand your people well and know what will work best with this unique group of individuals.
- When rolling out new changes, it is important to consider how they will affect trust.
- When possible, decisions should be made as close as possible to the "sharp end of the stick," where the work is performed.
- When you're asking people to buy into a decision, it's important to give them the opportunity to weigh in.
- Developing trust requires:
  - communication, honesty, vulnerability, transparency

- making sure everyone feels as if their voice is being heard
- consistent behavior over time
- others understanding the intent behind your actions, that is, that the *why* behind any changes is clearly understood by those affected by the change
- strong relationships

Questions to Consider

1. What percent of the total workforce trusts one another (e.g., their peers and boss, their employees, their colleagues in another department) and doesn't assume hidden agendas or malicious motivation?

2. On a scale of one to ten, with one indicating you have yet to begin and ten that you are great, how would you rate the trust element of your bridge?

Chapter Ten – Teamwork

In September of 1943, Hans Hedtoft, a member of the Danish Labor Party, received a disturbing call from the German Embassy in Denmark's capital city, Copenhagen. It was from a German naval attaché who, technically, was the enemy, for Nazi Germany had conquered and occupied Denmark three years before. But this enemy attaché grew alarmed when he learned that the Nazi secret police, the Gestapo, were planning to round up all of Denmark's Jewish people and send them to concentration camps, which many understood were really death camps. So, the German attaché called the Danish politician, who quietly spoke to leaders of the nation's some eight thousand Jews. Word also spread to the Danish underground and Danish people, who began notifying their Jewish neighbors.

Within days, over seven thousand Jews were moved into hiding in farmhouses, orphanages, churches, and even a bishop's house. They were aided by ordinary people, like an ambulance driver who, upon hearing the news, grabbed a Copenhagen phone book, circled the names he thought were Jewish and drove through the city, knocking on doors and warning the occupants to flee. He even put some in his ambulance and drove them to hospitals, where they were given fake diagnoses and admitted by friendly doctors to hide them.

The Jews, aided by the Danes, quietly made their way into hiding and from hiding to the coast, where they were put into small boats and motored or rowed to Sweden, which maintained an uneasy neutrality during the war and allowed the refugees to enter their country.

The Nazi roundup of Denmark's Jews took place, as planned, on October 1. But instead of finding eight thousand victims, they found only three hundred.

This was an incredible display of teamwork by the Danes, by some of their leaders and many of their regular folks, their farmers, fishermen, housewives, doctors, drivers, priests, and others. No careful preplanning had been conducted, no instructional seminars held, no focus groups consulted, no metrics devised. It was an amazing feat of teamwork by a team that had no opportunity to prepare, all the more amazing because the team wasn't a team at all, just a bunch of individuals who shared a vision and were willing to work together for a common goal. They did so at great personal risk, for they knew that if they were caught, they would be sent to a Gestapo jail or perhaps a concentration camp, and the chances of returning whole from either place were less than optimal.

Think about your organization. Do its members display this level of teamwork? Half as much? A quarter? A tenth? None at all?

It's teamwork that created the "Miracle on Ice," the shocking upset victory of the young, inexperienced, United States hockey team over the veteran, long-dominant Soviet Union team in the 1980 Olympics. Man-for-man, pound-for-pound, there was no way the Americans could win unless they worked together to overcome their obvious deficiencies.

It was teamwork under extreme, life-and-death pressure that made it possible for the Apollo 13 astronauts to return to Earth when an oxygen tank in their service module ruptured.

It was teamwork that make it possible for the Underground Railroad of mid-1800s America to help many enslaved people make their way to freedom.

And it is teamwork, along with trust, that makes the Navy Seals one of the most successful small-unit military forces in the world. The Seals value teamwork and trust so highly that they will take a recruit who is less physically capable but absolutely trustworthy and bound to the team over one who is incredibly physically capable but less concerned with trust and teamwork.

Team, or TEAM?

It's easy to create a team. Simply assign a couple of people to work together, and you have a team. But do you have teamwork? Not necessarily. You do have people sharing the workload, which is a good start. Or it might be, if that's what they're really doing rather than dumping all the work on one very eager (or unlucky) person.

Something more is required to turn people working on the same project at the same time in the same place into a real team. And that something is, essentially, the rest of the Bridge. Teamwork springs from leadership that inspires people to want to go above and beyond for the common goal, from a culture that says we're better together, from trust that management really means what it says, from focus *on* and *in*, from reinforcement, and more. When every single part of the Bridge comes together, it becomes possible for individuals to come together as part of a team—as part of their actual team, if they are assigned to one, and as part of the many teams represented by their task, shift, department, location, business unit, functional or technical area. This is what General Stanley McCrystal calls the "team of teams," with all individuals and teams working together to accomplish the organization's goals.

Everyone in your organization is by default a member of the larger team and, depending on how your organization is structured, other teams as well. That is the starting position for everyone, but how often do they really work together as a team? How often do they even see themselves as belonging to any team at all? Really see and feel themselves as belonging, not just knowing they belong because some manager said so or assigned them to work with some other folks?

And to what degree does the leadership of your organization view itself as being members of the larger team rather than as a totally separate unit?

If you, as a leader, work through all the other parts of the Bridge, your people will be primed to see themselves as members of the larger team, as well as all the other teams they may be on or assigned to.

Unfortunately, it's very easy to destroy teamwork. These are some of the common ways I've seen this done:

- restructuring without considering teamwork
- heavy-handed punishments
- unnecessary internal competition
- meaningless rules

- lack of investment, or outright disinvestment, in workers and teams—including not training or educating people how to behave as a team, lack of resources, lack of support to attend team meetings, and lack of support for what the team is trying to accomplish

Let's take a look at each of these.

Headless Restructuring Destroys Teamwork

I worked with an organization that had a regional approach to managing operations. While they had a general management area, many functions were done at remote locations, including customer service, dispatch, office administration, environmental, health and safety, and human resources and engineering. For business reasons, leadership decided to restructure and gather together some of these critical functions in a stand-alone division. So, for example, all of the customer service people were called in from the remote locations and put into what became a corporate call center. They no longer saw the local colleagues they used to see every day, no longer spoke with them, no longer swapped stories about work with them. What had been perceived as local families were disbanded, and the sense of camaraderie evaporated. As a result, the sense of teamwork with customer service reps and the other departments was greatly weakened.

Any time you reorganize, you risk damaging teamwork and established relationships.

Heavy-Handed Punishment Destroys Teamwork

It's sad but true that not all organizations' human resources or labor-relations managers consider teamwork before acting. Some still cling to the old mindset of, when something goes wrong, naming, blaming, shaming, and retraining the "bad person" rather than trying to figure out what led to the mistake, what allowed it to happen, and addressing that issue.

Any time you blame a person, you harm teamwork. Even if no one else is blamed, there's a good chance someone else will be offended. The blamed person's friend or colleague, maybe the union rep or perhaps the person's team may be upset and may feel that they also might be named, blamed, shamed, and retrained if they make a mistake.

For one client some years back, I worked out an agreement between plant management and the union to implement a particular process designed to improve reliability. Although we had laid out the general approach ahead of time, I wanted to tour the facility and adjust plans accordingly. So, I went out there to meet with leadership, chat with some workers, and otherwise get to know the place well.

As I was being led through the facility, we passed by the union communication board, and there was a man looking at us and pinning a piece of paper to the board. I had no idea who he was, so, after he left, we went to see what he had posted and were dismayed to see that it was essentially a brochure proclaiming that the workers should resist the new process I was there to develop and implement.

It turned out that a week or two prior to my visit, the company had disciplined a worker who was very popular with the others and was also a favored member of the union. The human resources department at this company had a heavy-handed approach to mistakes that usually angered rather than enlightened workers, and this time the union was going to extract revenge.

They did exactly that by posting propaganda against my new process, dragging their feet as it was rolled out, and otherwise impeding our progress.

It's important to remember that teamwork only flourishes when the entire Bridge works. If there's a lack of trust or bad relations anywhere on the Bridge, you will see a lack of trust or bad relations on the Teamwork Cable, and teamwork will suffer.

Unnecessary Internal Competition Destroys Teamwork

One of my clients had two plants, each producing the same product, which was a raw material the head company used in its own manufacturing process.

The parent company set up a system whereby the two plants, which were only about forty miles away from each other, competed to sell the raw material to the head company. This created a significant "us versus them" mentality, with the two plants pitting themselves against each other when they should have been cooperating for the good of the organization. Plant A should have been able to call Plant B and say something like, "Hey, we're running short of some supplies, can you send us some?"

If both plants saw themselves as members of the same team, Plant B would answer, "Sure, we have some extra, I'll send it over." Instead, they said, "No way!" and celebrated the fact that they were going to "beat" Plant A that month.

I've seen this happen many times. Once you set parts of an organization in competition with each other, you invite them to see each other as the enemy. It becomes shift versus shift, department versus department, plant versus plant. I have seen one shift sabotage the next to "win," and I've seen how some incentives to be the winning shift or department are so enticing that people are incentivized to manipulate, cheat, or steal.

Competition is great; it can be fun and a spur to excellence. But not when it sets one part of your organization against another or one person against another. Just imagine if your liver decided to "beat" your kidneys, or your lungs were determined to "win" by keeping all the oxygen for themselves.

Meaningless Rules Destroy Teamwork

An overabundance of rules, a problem in and of itself, can directly attack teamwork. This happened to one of my clients that built lab facilities. They were concerned about their rate of on-the-job injuries. We already knew that twenty percent or more of the injuries had to do with how people were lifting and carrying equipment. The obvious question was, why aren't people helping each other with heavy or awkward lifts?

It didn't take much observation to learn why. We would see, for example, an HVAC technician, putting in some duct work, ask a nearby electrician, "Can you give me a hand with this?"

The electrician would say, "I don't have any time on my work order." He might turn to another person and ask, "Do you have any time on your work order to help the HVAC guy?" But that person would also say no.

It turns out that this company had a work order system that held everyone accountable to the minute. You might have exactly fifteen minutes to accomplish this task, forty minutes for that assignment, one hundred minutes for the other job. Going over your time limit was not allowed, so you couldn't afford to lose time by stopping to help someone else.

When we took this finding to leadership, we learned that years ago, somebody asked, "On average, how long does it take for us to tear down and build these labs?" No one knew, so they decided to do a time study to figure out the overall average time as well as the average time for each segment of the work and each task.

The study was conducted simply to gain information and better manage their projects. But they never explained that to the workers or supervisors, who got the impression that you had to document your work to the minute and never go over the limit. Teamwork was eroded because no one wanted to get in trouble for exceeding the time on their work order, even if it meant leaving fellow workers in the lurch. Not only did this harm teamwork, it also contributed to twenty percent of the injuries that were caused by people not helping each other.

When I explained this to leadership, they said, "That's not what we meant." That was true, but if no one knows what you mean, they'll come up with their own meaning.

Lack of Investment Destroys Teamwork

Over the past several decades, two-tier pay schedules have come into prominence. This happens when, to save money, a company decides that all new hires will be paid less than existing employees, even though they are doing the exact same jobs. The new hires may also get less comprehensive health plans and, instead of a defined-benefit pension, receive contributions to their 401k plans.

These may be necessary cost-cutting measures, but they erode teamwork by setting up classes of workers and by increasing the feeling that the organization doesn't care about the new people. Here's how one hospital employee put it when Kaiser Permanente instituted a two-tier system during the COVID-19 lockdowns: "While we're saving the world, they're planning our demise, it seems," said Kim Mullen, a nurse at Kaiser South Bay in Los Angeles and a union official who helped organize the strike vote. "It's so insulting after all we've done, that they're being manipulative."[24]

When a two-tier system was instituted at Nabisco, Kellogg, John Deere and other companies, workers went on strike. Organizations must keep expenses under control. But when doing so, they should consider the cost in terms of damage to teamwork.

Cutting the pay and benefits of new hires is just one way that organizations can reduce their investment in their employees. They might also reduce their training budgets, opportunities for professional development, and incentives and rewards. All of this may be necessary, but it will give workers the feeling that they and leadership are no longer playing for the same team or that leadership doesn't care about them as individuals, and that can be dangerous.

Even seemingly minor disinvestments in workers can damage trust. A client with a workforce of about two hundred people had an incentive program they called "Donuts, Donuts, Pizza." If a team of employees performed discretionary items that plant management believed would contribute to the improvement of performance and culture, the team received donuts one morning. If they did even more things from a certain list they received donuts every day for a week. And if they did even more, they would be given a pizza party in addition to the donuts. This was certainly not the healthiest

---

[24] Ahiza Garcia-Hodges, "What Is the 'Two-Tiered Wage System' Fueling Worker Strikes?'" *CNBC News*, October 20, 2021, https://www.nbcnews.com/business/business-news/what-two-tiered-wage-system-fueling-worker-strikes-n1281938.

incentive program ever conceived, but it worked, driving discretionary effort.

This plant was part of a larger corporation, and one day corporate decided to right-size the incentive programs across the company. That is, they wanted to make sure that every location was spending the same amount on incentives. Their primary objective was to increase incentives in locations that weren't providing enough. Unfortunately, for this to work, locations that were spending lots on incentives had to spend less. As a result, the "Donuts, Donuts, Pizza" was significantly changed. The byproduct was that the employees who had been enjoying the donuts and pizza felt that the organization didn't care about them anymore. The amount of discretionary effort dropped significantly in certain areas.

Silent Failure

Lack of teamwork is obvious when defined teams fail to perform defined actions. The team tasked with planning a new program rollout, for example, may devolve to squabbling and backstabbing and quite obviously fail to perform.

That's a problem, but at least you know what's happening and can try to figure out why. More dangerous is the insidious breakdown in teamwork that occurs when people deliberately decide to try less. They may not be mad at anyone, they may not want to hurt the organization, but they've quietly decided to do only what it takes and no more. No longer go-getters, they become paycheckers.

This phenomenon, called "quiet quitting," "coasting," or something similar, slowly erodes teamwork and with it trust, culture, and every other part of the Bridge. It can even erode compliance when a formerly conscientious workers skips a step or two in order to get out by the end of the shift. They're not malicious, don't want to harm anyone, and get no secret thrill from breaking the rules. They just want to be out the moment the shift ends, not a second later.

Instant Teamwork

In 2017, a family of six was caught in a riptide off the beach in Panama City, Florida.[25] The family, which included their sixty-seven-year-old grandmother, was exhausted after struggling for a long time to fight their way back to the beach.

A crowd began gathering on the sand, but people feared to swim out to help because they might also be caught in the rip tide and go under. Then, Derek and Jessica Simmons, a husband and wife out for a day of fun with their family at the beach, noticed the crowd. Thinking the people were pointing at a shark, they went to investigate. When they learned that a family was out in the riptide, at risk of drowning, they began urging others to link arms and form a human chain that would stretch from the beach out to the drowning family.

---

[25] Richard Luscombe, "At Least 80 People Form Human Chain to Rescue Stranded Group in Gulf of Mexico," *The Guardian*, July 11, 2017, https://www.theguardian.com/us-news/2017/jul/11/80-people-form-human-chain-rescue-gulf-of-mexico-florida.

People were afraid but Derek and Jessica urged them on and soon, a human chain began forming and growing out into the ocean. The longer the chain grew, the further out Derek and Jessica, on their bodyboards, could go. They finally reached the family and passed them back along the chain, saving their lives.

Ordinary people voluntarily put their lives at risk to be a link in this chain. Despite their fear, despite their lack of training, despite the lack of an official leader, they put themselves at risk and worked together as a team because they shared a vision.

What will your people do for your organization?

Insights from Industry Leaders

I asked leaders from a number of industries—including for-profit, non-profit, and governmental—for their insights into teamwork. Specifically, I asked, Why is teamwork essential to accomplish your goals? What does excellent teamwork look like in action?

Here are some of their answers:

Kelvin E. Roth, vice president, environmental, health, safety, and quality, CF Industries

- Teamwork is where everyone has a common goal, they have a clear role to play in achieving that goal, and they support each other in ensuring the goal is achieved.

Marc Gilbertson, vice president and facility general manager, East Dubuque Nitrogen Fertilizers

- Operation of a very complex chemical process takes a very wide range of skills, some extremely focused. If any one area is weak, it forces the other, stronger areas to bear more load. Excellence in teamwork starts with humility and people who are more interested in the common goal than the personal one.

Francis Charbonneaux, infrastructure and risk manager, Essity Operations France

- Teamwork is essential to ensure that everyone is involved in the process and that everyone can give opinions and make proposals. Teamwork allows challenge and taking into account everyone's ideas. Teamwork also allows the culture to change.

Jared Matthias, vice president of executive accounts, ChampionX

- One-team approach: Pull in everyone involved, from functions to supply chain, sales and finance, to work through challenges or opportunities and/or unforeseen fires impacting business. Everyone who is a key stakeholder has a seat at my table and a voice. We're all accountable in a one-team approach.

Commander Richard H. Tetrev, US Navy (retired)

- In my twilight years in the Navy, I was assigned as the executive officer of Naval Air Station Brunswick Maine (NASB). There were more than thirty units that were attached to NASB that we supported. NASB, the command, had assigned approximately one thousand personnel (the base at that time had a total of 3,500 personnel), and out of the thousand, 350 were civilians, with the vast majority being in the union.

I need to preface this by saying prior to this time I had earned a master's degree in human resources development and was armed with all the tools of the trade, so to speak. And on the first morning, within fifteen minutes of sitting down at my desk, my secretary told me that the local National Association of Government Employees President would like a word with me.

He presented me with a ULP (unfair labor practice) violation against NASB. ULPs are the worst to deal with because those violations can result in fines well over $100,000, as opposed to grievances, which run in the $20,000 range.

The education I had from my master's degree paid huge dividends, and, working with the union over a period of about three years, we were able to negotiate a contract that lasted from 1995 until the base closed in 2011. And when I retired from the Navy and my job as executive officer in 1996, all ULPs and grievances were settled.

NASB was awarded the Malcomb Baldridge National Quality Award for Government organizations. The same year, Harley Davidson was awarded the Malcomb Baldrige Award for private industry. Both Harley and NASB were invited to participate as presenters in national conferences, one in Chicago and one in St. Louis, to share our stories.

Michael Middleton, safety and health director, Georgia Power

- The restoration efforts of Hurricane Katrina were a great example of teamwork. During Katrina, employees who typically had individual contributor roles were empowered to lead, and lead they did! What was modeled in 2005 is the epitome of employees being selfless teammates. Close your eyes for a second and imagine losing every single cherished possession—your home, your vehicles, your clothing, every tangible memory. Yet for the greater good you must become outwardly focused and partner in leading one of the most historic restoration efforts in American history.

  That's what's in the DNA of Southern Company employees—teamwork, selflessness, and a pride in that triangle like no other. Across this country, it's recognized that whether it's an ice storm, a hurricane, or whatever natural disaster, when our teammates show up, we will safely restore energy back into the lives of our customers, and we will do it together.

Jeff Bechel, safety manager, Cardinal FG

- Empowerment creates engagement. Empowering people to make decisions that directly affect them and their work instills a sense of ownership and pride. Taking this simple step can build camaraderie and teamwork between all levels of an organization and steer the company culture toward safety culture excellence.

Jeff Nee, vice president, operations, GATX Inc.

- Companies can often be penny wise and pound foolish in trying to minimize labor and salary costs and working conditions. It's critical to have a fully engaged workforce. Employees should feel pride in where they work and what they make. If they don't, you'll never have their full engagement.

Key Points about Teamwork

- Teamwork makes the seemingly impossible become a reality, for people can do extraordinary things when they share a vision.
- Any number of things can erode teamwork, including blaming, an overabundance of rules, two-tier pay schedules, reorganizations, and setting parts of the organization in competition with each other.
- Teamwork only flourishes when the entire Bridge works.
- If no one knows what your intentions are, they'll come up with what they believe are your intentions.
- When people deliberately decide to try less, teamwork suffers.

Questions to Consider

1. How clear is the vision of excellence across the organization?
2. On a scale of one to ten, with one indicating you have yet to begin and ten that you are great, how

would you rate the confidence in the teamwork element of your bridge?

Chapter Eleven – System Capacity to Prevent and Recover

In the 1920s and '30s, the French gave a lot of thought to the possibility of yet another war with Germany. Their long-time enemy had most recently invaded France in 1914, and the resulting conflict had taken a terrible toll on France's army, economy, and national psyche.

Midway through 1940 it became clear that Germany would again invade—it was simply a matter of when. Desperate to prevent a repeat of 1914, which led to four years of horrible bloodletting on French soil, the French had constructed a defensive system that ran the length of their eastern border, from the English Channel in the north all the way down to the Mediterranean Sea. The crux of this defense system was the Maginot Line, a powerful series of fortifications that ran along France's border with Germany.

State of the art, heavily fortified, equipped with powerful guns, with ample depth and redundancy to ensure resilience, the Maginot Line would allow a relatively small number of French soldiers to prevent the Germans from invading along their common border. Instead, the German army would be forced to go "over the top" of the line, to invade to the north, going through Belgium to get to northern France. The French would instantly know of the German attack on Belgium and would be able to determine how the invading forces were arrayed. The French army, which had already stationed troops on its border with Belgium, would use this information to position themselves as they moved into Belgium to meet the invasion. And since England, which was allied with France, had also pre-positioned troops on the French-Belgium border, the combined French-British force might be able to counterattack the invading forces, catching them at weak points and sending them crawling back to Berlin.

That was the plan. And it worked, to a point. The Germans were indeed forced to invade through Belgium, and the French and British armies moved into Belgium to meet the invaders. Everything went according to plan except for one little detail: the Germans had found a weakness in the French defenses.

The problem wasn't with the Maginot Line, which performed exactly as planned. It had to do with the Ardennes Forest, which runs along part of the border between France and Belgium, at the northern end of the Maginot Line. The forest was dense and didn't have enough roads for tanks and massed formations of soldiers. French military experts concluded that it would be impossible for the Germans to attack through the Ardennes Forest, so the French built much lighter defenses on their side of the forest. They were confident that between the forest and the modest defenses, any German attack would slow to a crawl, giving the French plenty of time to shift their troops in response.

Certain that they had done everything possible to prevent a repeat of the disaster of 1914, the French waited for the invasion. It soon came, but not in the way everyone expected. The Germans split their forces, sending part of their army through the non-forested part of Belgium, as expected. But they sent another part through the "impassible" Ardennes Forest. Everyone kept their eye on one part of the German Army but not the other, the one sneaking through the forest. It was a gamble that paid off handsomely as hundreds of German tanks suddenly roared out of the Ardennes onto French territory, brushed past the light defenses, smashed into surprised French and British forces from the side, sent the British running back to England, and forced the French to surrender after just six weeks of war.

Stunned and utterly defeated, the French wondered what had gone wrong. They had studied the situation for two decades and consulted the finest experts. Everyone who mattered agreed that their plan was sound. Yet the results were even worse than those of 1914.

In retrospect, it appears that the French never asked themselves a simple question: We have an incredible plan to prevent an invasion. But if our plan fails, how will we recover?

The French had built a robust system of prevention but had not built a system of recovery. It's true that a German blitzkrieg through the Ardennes Forest was "impossible." It's also true that the impossible happens in war. General George Washington accomplished the impossible in 1776, rowing his ragtag forces across the ice-filled Delaware River on a bitterly cold December night to surprise and defeat British mercenaries at Trenton. Emperor Napoleon used speed and daring as weapons, showing up with his army where everyone "knew" they should not be, catching his enemies by surprise and defeating them.

In war, as in business and organizational management, the only thing we know with certainty is that there is no certainty. The unexpected will occur, and if you're not prepared to recover from a disaster that you had no way of preparing for, you might as well start sewing a white flag.

Planning to prevent negative outcomes is a great start. But you must also plan to recover from the unexpected, the unimagined, even the impossible.

System Capacity to Prevent

I know a writer who often interviews people for his books and articles. He arrives at each interview with two pens, two writing pads for taking notes, and two small tape recorders. "If one pen or recorder fails or a pad runs out of paper" he says, "I have a backup." When this writer flies to meet and interview someone, he puts a clean shirt and set of underwear in his carry-on in addition to the clothes in his suitcase. As he explains, "If the airline loses my suitcase, I still have something to wear."

This is an example of system capacity to prevent and recover. His approach is sound: carry backup work tools, and when traveling transport sets of work clothing in two totally separate cases.

In simple terms, system capacity to prevent consists of all the effort put into preventing unwanted or undesired outcomes. We're all familiar with the system capacity to prevent steps we have to take with our computers. With many programs and apps, when you move to delete something, a message pops up asking if you really want to trash it. And when you pay a bill online, you're asked to confirm the amount and other information. Many people are annoyed by what they view as rigmarole, but it serves a very useful purpose: it prevents bad things from happening.

Unfortunately, we humans are very good at creating situations for bad things to happen. For example, we often cut toward ourselves rather than away, despite repeated warnings from our parents, elementary school teachers, and on-the-job trainers and supervisors. We drive while distracted, fail to save for retirement, procrastinate when we should be studying for the test, and try to bring in all the groceries at once: is it really a good idea to carry three heavy bags in one arm, and four in the other? If you go to YouTube and search for "people doing dumb things" or something similar, you'll find enough examples to make you wonder how our species has survived.

That's why every organization must create the system capacity to prevent bad things from happening. Exactly what you're trying to prevent varies from industry to industry and organization to organization. In a small writing business, the focus may be on preventing poor quality writing, late delivery, and plagiarism. In an organization that governs an entire country, such as the White House, the focus may be on preventing nuclear war, preventing a viral epidemic from crippling commerce, preventing favorite bills from being tied up in congress, and far too many other things to list.

My background is in safety, so let me give you an example of how an organization might build in the system capacity to prevent workplace injuries. This is NIOSH's hierarchy of controls,[26] which takes us through a series of steps:

- Elimination – Can we do the work differently? For example, can we stop using the toxic chemical altogether?
- Substitution – Can we find a safer way to do the work? For example, if we have to use a chemical, can we use a less toxic one?
- Engineering controls – If we're working next to a machine with lots of pinch points, for example, can we put in some guarding to create physical distance?
- Administrative controls – If we're working next to a cliff, for example, can we set a rule that says you must maintain a ten-foot distance from the edge of the cliff at all times?
- Personal protective equipment – If work is being conducted on scaffolding, for example, can we require everyone to wear hard hats and can we set up fall protection?

This hierarchy of controls is very good at preventing workplace injuries, and other approaches are very good at preventing bad things from happening in finance, human resources, customer service, and other areas. But you

---

[26] "Hierarchy of Controls," *Centers for Disease Control and Prevention*, last reviewed August 11, 2022, https://www.cdc.gov/niosh/topics/hierarchy/default.html.

can't always prevent everything, no matter how good your plans. What then?

System Capacity to Recover

The Old Testament tells the story of Joseph, a Hebrew sold by his brothers as a slave to a passing caravan who wound up being right-hand man to the Pharaoh of Egypt. Joseph won this position because he could interpret dreams. One night, the Pharaoh dreamt of seven fat cows emerging from a river, only to be devoured by seven very skinny, unhealthy-looking cows. Then he had a second dream in which he saw seven good ears of corn, on a stalk, being devoured by seven thin and blasted ears of corn.

Joseph was brought before the Pharaoh and asked what this meant. The Hebrew explained that Egypt would enjoy seven years of good harvests, followed by seven years of bad harvests and starvation. The solution to the impending disaster, he explained, was to gather up and set aside enough food in the good years to carry the kingdom through the bad years. Pharoah agreed, appointed Joseph as his right-hand man, and put him in charge of the effort to store food against the coming famine.

Joseph and the Pharoah realized that they could not prevent the bad event from happening, but they could set up a system of recovery. For that's what the food-storage program was, system capacity to recover from an unpreventable, devastating famine. Pharoah and Joseph identified and met the challenge at hand.

Every organization faces challenges, and even the biggest and most storied organizations have failed to meet them at times. Hostess Brands, Apple, Marvel, IBM, Best Buy, Converse, Delta Airlines, General Motors, Nokia, Continental Airlines, Polaroid, World Com, Merck, Pan-Am Airlines, Sears, JCPenney, and Eastman Kodak are among the many giants pushed to the edge by scandal, competition, internal strife, and other challenges.

Challenges come from every direction. They come from within the organization as workers routinely make mistakes and sometimes act mischievously, even malevolently. Machines malfunction and plans misfire. Extensive product-launch research is proven to be wrong—remember New Coke? Well-reasoned strategy can take an organization down the road to oblivion. Think of Kodak and its strategy of sticking with photographic film rather than embracing the underdeveloped, unwieldy, unproven, and at the time much more expensive technology of digital photography.

Challenges come from Washington in the form of new laws and regulations and from distant capitals in the form of tariff wars, unfair competitive practices, changes in currency valuation, and more.

Challenges come from changes in social values. Think of the producers of the movie *All the Money in the World* and the huge problem they faced when one of their stars, actor Kevin Spacey, was hit with charges of sexual harassment. It's sad to say that in days past, sexual harassment was tolerated. But today it is not, so the producers were forced to reshoot every single scene in which Spacey appeared with a new actor stepping in at the last moment and to do so in just eight days in order to make the scheduled release date.

Challenges come in the form of pandemics, technological advances, demographic changes, evolving customer tastes, and so much more.

All organizations are continually being challenged, directly or indirectly. We can prevent some of these challenges from harming us, but others we cannot. That's when we must switch from prevention to recovery.

Just as we can build in the capacity to prevent, we can build in the capacity to recover. Organizations do so, for example, by purchasing fire, theft, and business continuity insurance, cross-training employees, setting up computer and power backup systems, building in secondary hydraulics on aircraft, and more. We can take even larger steps toward recovery, such as preparing alternative supply chains in advance of a problem. I suspect many businesses that buy computer chips from manufacturers in Taiwan are doing that right now as China is making threatening noises aimed at the island nation. Should China blockade or invade Taiwan, the world's primary source of chips will be disrupted.

Unfortunately, companies or entire industries sometimes fail to set up recovery systems, even for challenges that were easy to predict. One of these is the loss of knowledge and skills in the workforce, which is happening now in the electric generation and power delivery sectors. When the Great Recession began in 2008, new housing and other construction fell off alarmingly.

Concerned about the loss of business, companies that provided electrical generation and delivery stopped hiring and training new employees. Now, fourteen years later, there's a huge knowledge and experience gap across the industry. There are people with more than twenty-five years' experience looking at retirement, and people with ten or fewer years' experience—and many in the "ten or fewer" group are really neophytes.

As the twenty-five-, thirty-, and forty-year folks leave, a lot of hard-earned knowledge and experience goes with them. This may not matter in routine situations, but when the unusual happens, when that problem that only pops up every fifteen years strikes, there will be precious few employees who have dealt with it in the past to deal with it now.

Creating the Capacity to Recover from the Unimaginable

Building in the system capacity to recover from known, predictable problems is one thing. What about building in the ability to recover from bad things you don't know about?

Eight US Presidents have died in office: four were slain by assassins, four succumbed to disease. Our current president is the forty-sixth to hold that office, which means that 5.75% of our presidents have passed away while leading our nation, a not inconsequential percentage. And half of those who died were assassinated, which means the country had absolutely no time to prepare for a change of leadership and had to make the change while grieving and in shock.

Our founders understood that we cannot prevent presidents from passing away while still in office, so they set up a system of recovery: the vice president. The recovery system was bolstered by the Presidential Succession Act of 1947, which provided for a series of replacements should presidents die, resign, be removed from office, or are otherwise unable to fulfill their duties. The vice president is, of course, the first to take over. Then comes the speaker of the house, president pro tempore of the senate, secretary of state, secretary of defense, attorney general, secretary of the interior, secretary of agriculture, secretary of commerce, secretary of labor, secretary of health and human services, secretary of housing and urban development, secretary of transportation, secretary of energy, secretary of education, secretary of veterans affairs, and, finally, secretary of homeland security. We now have eighteen replacements in all, eighteen opportunities to recover from the disaster of losing a sitting president.

In addition, one cabinet member is appointed the "designated survivor" during State of the Union speeches and other times when all the leaders of the executive branch of government convene. This person stays away should the unthinkable and unpredictable occur, should everyone at the event be killed or incapacitated. We don't know how or when that might happen, but we know it's possible, even if only in the most theoretical sense.

What challenges have you not considered and are not prepared to recover from? Suppose your competitor "invades through the forest"? Suppose your supply chain suddenly dries up, your customer base deserts you, or your funding is abruptly cut off? Suppose a deranged shooter shows up at your facility? Suppose you discover that top leadership has been cooking the books for years? Suppose a hurricane takes out your building, or you're hit with a ransomware attack?

Yes, those things couldn't possibly happen to your organization. But suppose they do? Asking yourself that question prepares you to recover from both the imaginable and the unimaginable.

Among the known challenges are disruptions in the supply chain, loss of knowledge, leadership failure, loss of good employees, and failure to ensure that work is performed consistently and as designed. We understand and can sometimes anticipate these challenges. We can't say exactly when, where, and how they will occur, but we can prepare to recover from these and other problems. Not too long ago, I was visiting a company I was advising. We gathered in a conference room and the meeting leader began by going around the room, asking questions like, "Who has been trained in CPR?" Then she said something to the effect of, "In case someone collapses, Frieda, you do CPR, Franklin, you call 911, and Freddy, you go out to meet the first responders." They knew they couldn't prevent someone from collapsing of a heart attack or other health problem during the meeting, but they were prepared to recover from that crisis.

Compare that to my experience at another organization near Washington, DC, where I was in a meeting in one of their power-generation buildings.

Suddenly, the room began shaking. We were all puzzled and frightened as things began bouncing around on desks and shelves. Then someone said, "It must be a boiler about to blow; let's get out of here!" So, we hurried through hallways to get outside, only to discover that the rattling had been caused by an earthquake. The best way to survive an earthquake is to stay in place and seek cover, to get under a strong table or cover yourself with blankets—you definitely do not want to run through hallways. But since earthquakes are rare in this part of the country, the company had not trained its people how to respond. They never said to themselves, "The odds of an earthquake striking are negligible, but suppose one happens?"

Asking "suppose" over and over again is the way to begin building your system capacity to recover. Yes, create plans to prevent the known bad things from happening. Then ask yourself, "Suppose it happens, anyway?" And ask yourself, "What things have I *not* prepared to prevent? How will I recover when they strike?" Notice that I say "when," not "if," for as we've learned in recent years, little is certain. Pandemics speed across the globe, crippling commerce in less than four months from the time the first case was registered. Weather patterns go haywire, drying up rivers used for commerce and sending fuel prices soaring.[27] Social values change, economies collapse, countries invade each other, and so much more.

---

[27] Julia Horowitz, "Extreme Heat is Slamming the World's Three Biggest Economies All at Once," *CNN*, August 18, 2022, https://www.cnn.com/2022/08/18/business/heatwave-global-economy/index.html.

Any and all of these things and a thousand more may challenge your organization.

Shaking the Bridge Away

We typically think of the bad things that we want to prevent, or recover from, as happening to specific domains:

- *workers*, as in on-the-job injuries
- *customers/clients/patients*, as in selling tainted food or giving bad financial advice
- *production*, as when a machine breaks
- *the public,* as in hackers breaking into your customer database and stealing passwords and other information
- *the environment*, as in a factory accidently releasing polluted air or dirty water
- *profits,* as might happen with the theft of company property or store merchandise

These are terrible things, but building in the capacities to prevent and to recover shouldn't stop with items such as these.

For our purposes, the capacity to prevent and recover goes beyond these to include the Bridge to Excellence, to our organizational culture, trust, teamwork, compliance, and every other part of the Bridge. It includes preventing bad things from happening to the Bridge and recovering when they do.

Back in 2016, news broke that Wells Fargo, one of our nation's leading banking institutions, had been creating fake accounts for years. Pressured by supervisors to open more and more accounts, employees took to inventing them. If, for example, a Wells Fargo customer had a checking account, an employee would open a savings account and a credit card account for the same customer, without that customer's knowledge or consent. It's been estimated that Wells Fargo created 3.5 million unauthorized accounts, with as many as 190,000 of their customers being hit with various fees for accounts they didn't know they had.[28]

When this became public, Wells Fargo responded by blaming low level employees as well as supervisors for not paying attention to what was happening. But the true problem was rooted in leadership which, while proclaiming that its vision was to "satisfy our customers' financial needs,"[29] was demanding that workers open more and more accounts, then turning a blind eye to any wrongdoings.

You can imagine how this shook the Wells Fargo Bridge to Excellence and how the Bridge was forcefully shaken again and again as the bank was forced to lay off thousands of employees, admit to additional bad practices regarding mortgages and auto loans, and pay billions of dollars in fines. When CNN asked Wells Fargo employees

---

[28] Uri Berliner, "Wells Fargo Admits to Nearly Twice as Many Possible Fake Accounts – 3.5 Million," *NPR*, August 31, 2017.
https://www.npr.org/sections/thetwo-way/2017/08/31/547550804/wells-fargo-admits-to-nearly-twice-as-many-possible-fake-accounts-3-5-million.
[29] Wells Fargo & Company Annual Report 2015,
https://www08.wellsfargomedia.com/assets/pdf/about/investor-relations/annual-reports/2015-annual-report.pdf.

how they felt about this, the responses included the following:[30]

- "It's beyond embarrassing to admit I am a current employee these days. My family and friends think I'm a fraud for working at Wells," said John, a home mortgage consultant for Wells Fargo.
- "They don't care about us. All they care about is money in their pocket," said Jane, a Wells Fargo collections worker who is being treated for depression and anxiety due to the high-stress work environment.
- "We have been dragged through the mud. We have been outright blamed by our CEO," said Sandra, who works at a Wells Fargo call center.

My point is not to disparage Wells Fargo for its lapses. Rather, it is to point out that what happens within an organization affects its Bridge. When leadership tells the workers one thing—as in, "Satisfy our customers' financial needs"—but pressures them to do another—as in, "Sell, sell, sell!"—it alters the organization's culture by forcing employees to lie and cheat. Workers can no longer believe in the organization's stated values, cannot respect leadership, and cannot trust management. After all, they may be fired for *not* breaking the rules, but then, if a sacrificial victim is needed, they may be fired for breaking them.

---

[30] Matt Egan, "Inside Wells Fargo, Workers Say the Mood Is Grim," *CNN Business*, November 3, 2016, https://money.cnn.com/2016/11/03/investing/wells-fargo-morale-problem/index.html.

Trust between leadership, management, and workers is all but severed. So is the trust between individual workers, who wonder why the person sitting or standing next to them is willing to go along with this—or refusing to—and whether that person will rat them out.

Teamwork is destroyed as the organization becomes siloed into areas that break the rules, areas that do not, and areas not directly affected but that know what's going on.

Compliance is twice eroded: first, because employees break certain rules, and second, because they presume that, since management wants them to break these rules, other rules must be breakable as well.

During the several years it took for the Wells Fargo scandal to play out, the company suffered a significant drop in business and stock price, was forced to pay big fines, and was hit with restrictions regarding capitalization and growth. While it's CEO was forced to resign, most other leaders remained in place, and some were promoted. Given the significant damage to its culture, trust, compliance, and the rest of its Bridge, how much excellence was Wells Fargo capable of producing? How many employees were eager to go above and beyond, and were the best and the brightest in the industry eager to work for the bank?

Recovery by Maintenance, Twice at Once

The goal is to prevent and to recover from bad things that happen to the organization's activities, as well as from bad things that happen to its Bridge. Sometimes, these go hand in hand. Imagine a company that has sailed along for years and suddenly a new competitor arises and steals away a significant chunk of business. The company suffers from a loss of sales and profits. If leadership responds by laying off a bunch of workers, the Culture Pillar, Trust Truss, and Teamwork Cable will be weakened and the entire Bridge shaken.

In this case, problems that began outside the company spread to its Bridge. Sometimes it works the other way around, as with Wells Fargo, where the problem began internally as leadership demanded its workers meet impossible goals. No matter where a problem begins, however, there's a good chance it will eventually envelop both the organization and its Bridge.

You can prevent this "double damage" and set the conditions for recovery by performing constant maintenance on your organization and on its Bridge.

There are different types of maintenance. There's reactive maintenance, in which you repair something that has gone wrong. For example, the engine in the company truck fails and you fix it.

There's predictive maintenance, which might take the form of changing the truck's oil every so many miles. We do so because we can predict there will be a problem if the oil gets too old.

There's maintenance based on usage, as in changing the spark plugs every so many miles, and maintenance based on time, as in changing the filter in your heating system every so many months.

Your organization and its Bridge require constant preventive and reactive maintenance of all types. You must continually go round and round your organization and its Bridge asking important questions: What can we maintain? Is this a sign of impending trouble? Suppose it happens, despite all our plans?

Are there hairline cracks in our culture? If so, what form of maintenance should we do?

Have we recently performed predictive maintenance on the Trust Truss? For example, have we made sure that our top leaders really know what's happening in the organization? Or are they locked into private offices, private conference rooms, private lunchrooms, private bathrooms, and private entrances to such a degree that they have no idea what's happing outside their bubble, no idea if their plans and priorities are being distorted, and no idea whether workers think leadership is good or a joke or a toxic presence?

Constant, multi-faceted maintenance helps ensure that human resources, production, legal, transportation, and all the other departments—plus all the individuals in those departments—are doing what they are supposed to be doing. At the same time, it helps keep your Bridge strong. Remember, your organization and its Bridge are one and the same. For the sake of convenience, we talk about the organization's activities and its Bridge separately, but they are the same. They're just different ways of viewing, understanding, and guiding the organization.

When the organization's activities go askew, the Bridge will as well. The reverse is also true. If the Bridge is rocked, activities will be upset.

Restoring Health

Constantly performing maintenance of all types on your organization and on your Bridge is the best way to prevent bad things from happening and to recover when they do.

You can't prevent all bad things from happening, for there's a limit to how much time, money, and effort you can devote to prevention. And even if your plans are perfect, you can be sure something will catch you by surprise and rock your organization. But if you spend the time, money, and effort to continually maintain both your organization and your Bridge, you will be much better fortified against bad things happening, and much better prepared to recover when they strike.

During the COVID-19 pandemic, scientists around the world raced to a develop a system to prevent the disease from sickening people. That system took the form of vaccines. But the global community didn't stop at prevention. It also worked aggressively to develop medical treatments to help those who contracted the disease. They carefully tried out different medicines, monitored the efficacy of ventilators, and more. While early detection and early response is the mantra of healthcare, we must also have systems of care available to restore to good health those who do become ill or injured. The same applies in business. You cannot prevent all unwanted events. Do everything you can to head them off and, at the same time, develop the means to restore the organization to health, just in case.

Insights from Industry Leaders

I asked leaders from a number of industries—including for-profit, non-profit, and governmental—for their insights into the common failures their business or industry might experience, as well as their system capacity to prevent and system capacity to recover.

With respect to managing failure, I asked: What are some examples of common failures your type of business or industry might experience?

Here are some of their answers:

Kolin Ibrahim, senior manager, environmental, health, and safety, Hess Corporation

- Production losses
- Safety injury, loss of containment
- Blaming people for mistakes
- Wasted time and money
- Regulatory citations for non-compliance

Tobias Read, founder, AQRA Group

- Failure to follow client agreements which can lead to fines, cancelled contracts, and even legal action
- Failure to follow human resource processes and FLSA rules, which can lead to individual or collective actions, which can be potentially damaging, time consuming, and potentially very expensive

- Failure to adhere to professional guidelines, which can lead to fines, legal issues, and reputational damage

Kelvin E. Roth, vice president, environmental, health, safety, and quality, CF Industries

- Over confidence; over reliance on a single source of control

Kirk Bagnal, owner, Ethostory

- Just like any organization, the ones that I have been a part of have a myriad of failure modes and ongoing errors, mistakes, failures, and experiences that simply do not live up to expectations. Taiichi Ohno stated, "All companies have problems. In fact, they have endless problems. The ones that know their problems early are the ones that win." Our advantage is that we can see our errors quickly *and* we have fought tirelessly to get out of the blame cycle. Often, when a failure occurs, organizations (even the ones that I've led, I confess) respond poorly by jumping quickly into the blame cycle, which goes like this: human error occurs >> individual is counseled or disciplined >> reduced trust >> less communication >> management becomes less aware of jobsite risks and conditions >> organizational weaknesses persist >> defenses become flawed >> when the *next* human error occurs, it happens to be a critical active error, and there is a mission critical unwanted outcome. So, as you can see, there are two key steps: (1) knowing errors quickly, and (2) getting *out* of the blame cycle and promoting a culture of transparency, trust, and resilience where blame is not the norm—rather, learning is the norm. I like to think of it this way: the opposite of blame is learning. We don't jump to blame; we dig to learn.

Joel Simon, partner, Fernelius and Simon

- Failing to communicate is the biggest issue in my line of work. Surprises happen, but I have found that many surprises can be avoided by leaders and employees taking ownership of tasks and realizing that they are not alone in handling issues when they arise.

Mike Diezi, executive director, Spec's Wine, Spirits & Finer Foods

- This industry is heavily regulated and is under constant surveillance. One of the most common potential failures this industry may experience is not properly checking to ensure that a customer is of the proper age. Regulatory agencies check regularly to ensure compliance. We focus on training the staff on the proper way to manage the situation and to avoid any violation. I am very proud to report that we are checked multiple times on a very regular basis across the state and have always done very well in this area. This is attributed, again, to training and *communication*.

Michael Middleton, safety and health director, Georgia Power

- Failures in the power industry throughout the country have made headlines over the past few years, so most people are already aware of them. What I think is important for our industry is that we focus on how we handle those failures and how we can prevent them in the future. The ability to be vulnerable as we acknowledge failure and demonstrate a strong passion to foster a culture of continuous improvement is unique, yet if not demonstrated by the highest levels it will stifle an organization.

There are some significant leadership perspectives that I often reflect on:

1. "Are you okay? Are they okay?" What powerful questions! But should we wait until a serious event to ask them? This takes intentional work and requires you knowing your teammates, but these simple, yet powerful, questions are foundational and help avoid failures.

2. How will you handle or how have you handled your "defining moments?" Do you take time to ponder this question? You can never stop working on safety. Putting yourself and your team in different scenarios to plan ahead and strategize is worth the intentional time.

3. What's the pulse of your safety culture? How do you know?

4. You probably are taking it home, but should you? Reflecting on negative events sometimes takes a toll on me, and not just professionally. An acknowledgement that you may not always be able to separate work and life is important. As we shift to more virtual work, these lines will continue to get blurrier. Be careful!

5. Are you outwardly focused? Significant events can have a ripple effect, and as a leader it's important to constantly reassess who else needs to know, who this is impacting, and why and how.
6. Be deliberate! Are you willing to make a decision, even if you don't have all the information?

With respect to system capacity to prevent, I asked: What are some examples of systems you have to prevent undesirable outcomes, not just injuries?

Here are some of their answers:

Mark Kehne, plant manager, Cardinal FG

- Our facility is to ISO 9001:2015 (quality management system) certified. As such, we have built in preventive systems to ensure that our raw materials meet our specifications, our production process operates within our established acceptable targets, our product quality meets our customers' needs, and our inventory management ensures that orders are fulfilled on time. Throughout these steps of our operation, we have both machine and human-based auditing steps to ensure that the preventive systems are functioning properly. In the rare event of a result that is outside of the acceptable tolerance in any of these areas, we utilize root cause analysis and corrective action tool kits to close any gaps.

Tobias Read, founder, AQRA Group

- This is perhaps different for human-capital-based businesses, where the issues are not typically critical equipment failure or fatalities in a plant. However, there can be negative or undesirable outcomes with customers, employees, suppliers, and so on. To mitigate this requires leadership to do the following:
  - o Set a very clear cultural identity, but make sure that this is collectively owned, not centrally imposed. Also, when new staff join, "Sheep Dip" and train in all elements of the culture.
  - o Enable the culture to raise issues without retribution so that failures don't happen.
  - o Conduct external audits. For example, audit account compliance to the legal contracts, quality of service to the service level specifications.
  - o Try to provide proactive training. Train staff on issues before they become an issue, not just after the horse has left the stable.

Kelvin E. Roth, vice president, environmental, health, safety, and quality, CF Industries

- I'm baffled why we only talk about layers of protection in process safety but not in the personal safety realm. We have systems like training, coaching, procedure, and checklists that are designed to prevent undesirable outcomes. But we need to think of them in layers. We know that neither systems nor people are perfect, and we need to stop pretending that they are. Even in simple tasks, have you talked through plans A, B and C? You may be positive you'll never need plan C, but if you're ever faced with a situation requiring it, you'll be ready to implement it.

- The hierarchy of controls is often viewed as "which ONE of these should we do?" rather than "how many can we do/should we do?"

Chris Boleman, president and chief executive officer, Houston Livestock Show and Rodeo

An undesirable outcome is not learning from a failure and continuing to fail over and over again. Now, from an injury perspective, in my line of work, it is all about testing and ensuring you have conducted appropriate risk assessments.

Kirk Bagnal, owner, Ethostory

- The combination of a sound and sustained 5S Process (a workplace organization method that focuses on sorting, setting in order, shining, standardizing, and sustaining) with a deeply ingrained human performance improvement (HPI) process equips any organization to build the foundation of becoming a high reliability organization, making them pre-eminent (best of the best) in their industry.

Mike Diezi, executive director, Spec's Wine, Spirits & Finer Foods

- Each industry has its challenges. Some are similar across the board, and some are unique. Retail always has the risk of shrink from theft. The liquor industry indexes higher in this category than most other retail operations.

- We have a fantastic loss prevention department that has proven to be successful in preventing or catching this activity.
- Their chainwide communication can also alert stores and have local law enforcement at the ready. There are other procedures that have proven extremely successful but cannot be discussed as that would risk a reduction of their effectiveness. Suffice it to say that, once again, communication makes these processes successful.

Najya Al Hinai, continuous improvement lead, MSEML

- One generic tool used across the organization is the visual management board for our critical systems. It's a visualization of the end-to-end process, be it for deployment of a program, or day-to-day operational work. It allows us to understand where our potential shortfalls are prior to them becoming a problem or incident. This way we can reflect and amend our processes to avoid such failures in the future.

With respect to system capacity to recover, I asked: What are some examples of systems that you have that "kick in," or in other words, start up when mistakes or deviations from expected outcomes occur?

Here are some of their answers:

Kolin Ibrahim, senior manager, environmental, health, and safety, Hess Corporation

- emergency response process
- production deferral process
- defect elimination process

Mark Kehne, plant manager, Cardinal FG

- Our process operates twenty-four hours per day, seven days per week, 365 days per year for ten to twenty years between scheduled downtime. In order for this to happen, by necessity we have backup systems for all critical elements of the operation including raw materials and feed system, processing equipment, utilities, and manning strategies. Our priorities are to first, preserve the process, second, to preserve the product stream, and lastly, to preserve the quality of the product—all without risk to our employees or to our facility.

Tobias Read, founder, AQRA Group

- Assign your best people to immediately investigate and report back. They may be senior managers, people from other locations, or internal auditors.
- Communicate quickly, comprehensively, and honestly to your client, painful as it may be. I've always found that clients will give you a second chance if you keep them fully involved. If they find out via the grapevine, then that can lead to major problems. Keep them informed as a situation develops.
- Once a solution is found, institutionalize the knowledge and if severe, conduct deep retraining to avoid reoccurrence.

Kelvin E. Roth, vice president, environmental, health, safety, and quality, CF Industries

- We talk about business continuity, but have we thought about safety continuity? In business continuity, we use "assess, prevent, respond, recover, and restore." All those same phases apply at a smaller scale with safety. Also, business continuity acknowledges that there is no perfection, so it's about minimizing impact and bouncing back stronger. How refreshing that would be if we talked about safety in those same terms.

Chris Boleman, president and chief executive officer, Houston Livestock Show and Rodeo

- In our line of work, it is really about having the appropriate in-house expertise and consultants ready to react if a problem happens. We are very strategic in having crisis management plans in place, and we conduct table-top exercises as a piece of training for our team and the folks that partner with us during events.

Ed Senavaitis, director of corporate safety, Buckeye Partners, LP

- We are willing to look at our systems and processes as potential contributing factors. We tend to look outward much more easily that we look inward.

Mike Diezi, executive director, Spec's Wine, Spirits & Finer Foods

- During the COVID-19 lockdown and public health challenges we were faced with many situations that needed immediate responses. The retail operations field team was fantastic. Human resources had a full protocol for any incident so that a store could be sterilized, and the personnel and guests could return to a safe environment. While so many companies had to halt operations and jobs were lost, Spec's was able to safely remain open, allowing our associates to maintain their earnings and avoid financial hardship. This required employees to be flexible and pivot. If a store discovered a virus-positive associate or a guest had potentially exposed a store, that location had to be cleared and sanitized. While that location was working through the protocol, healthy employees would have to work at a different location. In summary, our system is entirely dependent upon our people to be flexible and stay in constant communication to understand the challenge. Properly inspired associates who feel heard through open, two-way communication are positively motivated to handle any situation. Our people are our system to recover. With the right team and the right attitude, no challenge cannot be overcome.

Key Points about Your System Capacity to Prevent and Recover

- Planning to prevent negative outcomes is a great start. But you must also plan to recover from the unexpected, the unimagined, and even the impossible.
- All organizations are continually being challenged, directly or indirectly. We can prevent some of these challenges from harming us, but others we cannot. That's when we must switch from prevention to recovery.
- Asking "suppose" over and over again is the way to begin building your system capacity to recover.

- Your organization and its Bridge require constant preventive and reactive maintenance. You must continually go round and round your organization and its Bridge asking, What can we maintain? Is this a sign of impending trouble? Suppose it happens, despite all our plans?
- Do everything you can to head problems off and, at the same time, develop the means to restore the organization to health, just in case.

Questions to Consider

1. On a scale of one to ten, with one indicating you have yet to begin and ten that you are great, how would you rate your confidence in your system capacity to prevent undesirable outcomes?
2. On the same scale of one to ten, what score would you give for your confidence in your system capacity to recover from undesirable outcomes?

Chapter Twelve – It's All about Engagement

Hurricane Ian recently cut a nasty swath of destruction through Florida and nearby states, with damages estimated to be greater than $50 billion.[31] The deaths of 132 Americans made Ian the deadliest hurricane since Katrina in 2005. Ian also damaged bridges, such as the Sanibel Causeway, which carries vehicles from the Florida mainland to Sanibel Island. Portions of the bridge collapsed and were washed away.

I don't know how well the Sanibel Causeway was cared for, what its maintenance budget was, or how often it was inspected. I do know, however, that the current bridge was completed in 2007. This means it stood for only fifteen years, which is much less than the fifty or so years bridges are usually engineered to stand.

Living on the Gulf Coast of the United States and having seen my own home flooded by Hurricane Harvey in 2017, I know all too well that the paths hurricanes take and the damage they cause is unpredictable. But the fact that hurricanes blow bridges over is not. Neither is anyone surprised to learn that hurricanes have and will continue to blow through the southeastern US, or that tornadoes, floods, and earthquakes will strike in other parts of the country, and that all this wind, water, and earth movement will put terrible strains on our bridges, old and new.

---

[31] "Hurricane Ian Is 15th Billion-Dollar Disaster of The Year," *The Weather Channel*, October 11, 2022, https://weather.com/news/weather/video/hurricane-ian-is-15th-billion-dollar-disaster-of-the-year.

Hurricane, tornado, flood, and earthquake damage to bridges is certain, while damage and disruption caused by ships, trains, and trucks plowing into bridge supports on water and land is nearly certain. We can also predict that unhappy people will climb upon bridges to commit suicide, that protestors will take over bridges and stop traffic, that landslides will damage or demolish bridge supports, and more.

Other problems are less predictable. For example, San Francisco's Golden Gate Bridge has seen three women give birth on its roadway, an escaped six-foot-tall ostrich run across it and stop traffic, and Canadian engineering students hang a Volkswagen Beetle off its side late one night.

There are problems caused by a combination of predictable and unseen factors. Engineers take the weight of people into account when building bridges, but sometimes fail to predict the reasons why a human overload might occur and don't strengthen the bridge accordingly. In 1444, Venice's Rialto Bridge collapsed when too many wedding guests crowded onto it. Other bridges have failed when too many people climbed on to view a baptism, watch a clown go down the river in a barrel, and participate in a funeral procession.

Then there are surprises coming from the sky. Airplanes have made emergency or crash landings on New York's George Washington Bridge, Miami's Haulover Inlet Bridge, and others.

There's also fire damage. Bridges have been deliberately set on fire by arsonists and accidently by fireworks. In 2001, a fuel tanker passing under the I-285 Bridge in Atlanta, Georgia, overturned and caught fire, with the flames quickly engulfing the bridge above. In 2022, a fire that started in a homeless camp rose to enflame the bridge overhead.

And, of course, human greed has doomed more than a few bridges. For example, in 2007, China's Tuo River Bridge collapsed because, it is believed, the contractor used shoddy materials in construction.

Human anger poses another threat. According to an analysis produced by the Bridge Engineering Software & Technology Center at the University of Maryland, "Transportation facilities are attractive targets for terrorists because they are easily accessible, and an attack could have considerable impact on human lives and economic activity. This is especially true for transportation assets such as bridges."[32] And indeed, immediately following 9/11, credible threats were launched against the Golden Gate Bridge, the Vincent Thomas Bridge in Los Angeles, and San Diego's Coronado Bridge.[33]

Then there is perhaps the least predictable event, with bridges falling down as they are being built. This

---

[32] "Risk Analysis for Explosive Attacks on Highway Bridges," BEST Center, https://best.umd.edu/risk-analysis-for-explosive-attacks-on-highway-bridges/.
[33] Duncan Campbell, "Terrorist Alert at California Bridges," *The Guardian*, November 2, 2001, https://www.theguardian.com/world/2001/nov/02/september11.usa1.

happened to Australia's West Gate Bridge in 1970, Denmark's Fiskenbaekbroen Bridge in 1972, Japan's Astram Line bridge in 1991, China's Baikong Railway Bridge in 1996, Spain's Almunecar Motorway Bridge in 2005, Russian's Yekaterinburg Bridge in 2006, and others.

I'm not trying to scare you away from ever using a bridge again. Instead, I want to make it clear that every bridge of every sort in every place and in every time faces challenges and stress. Sometimes the problems come from within, as when engineers err in their calculations or contractors use shoddy materials. Sometimes the problems come from without, as with babies being born, clowns in barrels, fires, and fiery crashes. Sometimes the problems are acts of God, as in hurricanes; sometimes acts of anger, as in terrorism; and sometimes acts of disturbed minds, as with arson.

Every physical bridge is vulnerable. And every metaphorical Bridge to Excellence is just as vulnerable. The only way to prevent damage to your Bridge and to recover from unpreventable damage is constant diligence and vigilance.

You don't want to be Chicken Little, predicting that the sky will fall every time an acorn drops on your head. But you do want to constantly patrol and inspect your Bridge, honesty assessing its strengths and weaknesses—and yours' as well—then act accordingly.

Your Bridge "Metric"

More than forty-three thousand physical bridges in the United States are in poor condition.[34] Fortunately, we have tools to identify problems with physical bridges before they occur. But how do you assess the integrity of your metaphorical organizational Bridge to Excellence?

Perhaps the best way is to think of your Bridge as being a factory. It uses the inputs of trust, leadership, teamwork, culture, and other parts of the Bridge to create the output of strong employee engagement (See Diagram 1).

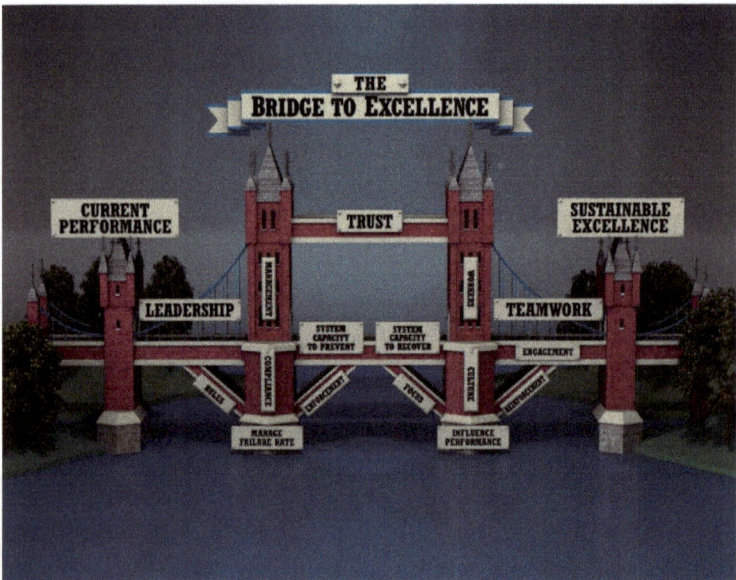

Diagram 1: The Bridge to Excellence

[34] Alison Premo Black, "2022 Bridge Report," American Road & Transportation Builders Association, https://artbabridgereport.org/.

Employee engagement, simply put, is the emotional commitment and level of buy-in, participation, and ownership that an employee feels toward their work and the company they work for. The higher the level of engagement, the better for the organization. Workers who are not engaged participate in the work but with little emotional interest or desire to be involved in anything extra. And workers who are outright disengaged are emotionally detached, disinterested, and withdrawn. They barely meet the minimum expectations of work performance.

Ideally, your "factory" will produce high levels of employee engagement, for that's what it takes to excel over a long period of time through the trials and tribulations that assail us all. Indeed, if you were to select a single item to stand in for the health of your bridge, it should be employee engagement.

Unfortunately, many organizations are hamstrung by weak employee engagement, non-engagement, or outright disengagement. According to some experts, seventy percent of American workers are not actively engaged in their jobs. According to others, engagement had been trending upwards, but fell during the COVID-19 pandemic. We are still working to understand the impact of the virus on global commerce, and how long it will last. But both pre- and post-COVID-19 data should alarm leaders and prompt them to work to understand the motivators that exist within their organizations.

Understanding these motivators is crucial for, worldwide, workers who are not engaged or are actively disengaged cost $7.8 billion in lost productivity.[35] This equals 11% of the world's GDP.

According to a Gallup analysis of over 110,000 business units, when you compare teams in the top quartile of employee engagement to those in the bottom quartile, you find that the top teams deliver the following:

- 10% higher customer loyalty/engagement
- 23% higher profitability
- 18% higher productivity (sales)
- 14% higher productivity (production records and evaluations)
- 18% lower turnover for high-turnover organizations (those with more than 40% annualized turnover)
- 43% lower turnover for low-turnover organizations (those with 40% or lower annualized turnover)[36]

Here's another way to look at the value of engagement. I don't know any more about the current war in Ukraine than what is broadcast by the media, but it seems clear that the Ukrainian soldiers are highly motivated and fully engaged in their duties, while the Russians soldiers are less so or not at all. This lack of engagement cancels out many of the Russian military advantages. Yes, the Russians began the war with more

[35] Ryan Pendell, "The World's $7.8 Trillion Workplace Problem," Gallup Workplace, June 14, 2022, https://www.gallup.com/workplace/393497/world-trillion-workplace-problem.aspx.

[36] Ryan Pendell, "The World's $7.8 Trillion Workplace Problem," Gallup Workplace, June 14, 2022, https://www.gallup.com/workplace/393497/world-trillion-workplace-problem.aspx.

tanks, troops, airplanes, and other assets. These numerical advantages are important and may finally prove to be the deciding factor. But so far, the outnumbered, outgunned, yet highly engaged Ukrainians are punching well above their weight.

Getting Engaged

Much has been written on the art and science of engaging workers. Approaches vary from organization to organization, industry to industry, leadership approach to leadership approach, but increasing engagement boils down to ensuring employees buy into their work and the direction of the business, are able to participate in efforts to improve, and have a true sense of ownership in the work being performed.

You can't expect all workers to become engaged on their own, out of the blue. Yes, there will be those who self-engage, but they're only one of the five types of employees you can expect to have.

The first are the pioneers, the mavens, the people who walk in your door excited about your organization and what you do. They're like the people who camp outside of Apple stores so they can be the first to have the newest device. They want to be part of every initiative, they want to share their excitement with others, and they're always willing to go above and beyond.

Second are the "yes" people, although I don't mean this in a derogatory way. They're the ones who, if asked, "Hey Jake, this is what we're thinking of doing, and here's why. Would you mind helping us out?" will quickly reply, "Sure! What do you need?" They're probably not going to be the first to volunteer, but if you ask them and give them the rationale, they're happy to go above and beyond.

Third are the crowd followers, those who wait until they see what others are doing. When "doing it this way" becomes part of the culture and everybody else is "doing it this way," they will happily go along. They want to fit in. If you move the culture in the right direction, you move them as well.

Fourth are the skeptics. They tend to mistrust missions, and view value/mission statements as propaganda. They're not concerned about what others are doing or thinking. They need to see the raw, hard data to be convinced.

Fifth and final are the CAVE people, the "Citizens Against Virtually Everything." They will probably never take your organization's goals and dreams to heart. They may do good work as a matter of personal pride, but they have absolutely no intention of going above and beyond. In addition, they are opposed to any new changes and have a steadfast distrust of management's actions and intentions.

Your pioneers are already highly engaged in their work. On the other hand, the CAVE folks are likely firmly disengaged. No matter what you do or say, no matter what incentives you offer or punishments you level, they will remain "paycheckers."

This means that the "yes" folks, crowd followers, and skeptics are your best veins to mine—and there are a lot of them in every organization. They're like the big middle section on the bell curve. While your pioneers embrace your goals and your CAVErs scoff at them, the "yesers," crowd followers, and skeptics aren't paying much attention to them. They need the nudge, or to see what others are doing, or to look at the cold, hard data.

You, as a leader, need to understand your people, what category they fall into, how to influence their performance, and what will increase their motivation and engagement. It's not just a matter of offering more money, for that has relatively short staying power as a persuasion device. The bonus or higher salary quickly becomes the new norm or expectation rather than a motivation. Instead, you need to understand what matters to your people. You can do this by doing the following, among other things:

- *Learn what they're doing* – Spend time with them in their work areas to understand what helps and hinders them from performing their tasks with satisfaction. A little "management by wandering around" can go a long way.
- *Skip a rung* – Some of my clients hold skip-level meetings to build trust and ensure effective communication. For a skip, the boss's boss meets directly with employees without their first-line boss in attendance. Properly done, this gives the boss's boss access to unfiltered information and an opportunity to really understand what's happening

within the organization. Other clients expect their leaders to meet one-on-one with subordinates to discuss performance results, resolve issues, and build stronger teams, communication, and commitment.

- *Ask the "experts"* – An organization's employees are not just customers and consumers of the various initiatives to improve performance and culture. They are also the best problem-solvers within the organization, because they're at the sharp end of the stick, the point where initiatives designed at headquarters leap off the page and meet reality. This gives your employees a great deal of insight into what does and does not work.

- *Enlist informal leaders* – Every organization has informal leaders, people whom the others look to for direction despite the fact that these folks lack formal titles or positions. Informal leaders often have a powerful influence on culture, which gives them powerful influence over any changes proposed by leadership. Before initiating changes, it behooves leadership to share their tentative plans with these influencers to gain their perspectives and eventually their support. Leadership can then check in with these individuals as the change is executed to learn how the workers perceive and are responding to the change.

- *Show that you care about what matters to them* – For most people, the primary thing in life is their family. Here's a little thought exercise. Think of three people in your organization whose level of engagement you would like to influence. Think of their names. Picture their faces. Now, can you name their family members? If so, you've probably chatted with them about their family members and created the impression that you care enough to get to know who is important to them. But if you cannot name the names, you may have unintentionally created the impression that you do not care enough about them. People take many cues from the boss. If an employee thinks the boss genuinely cares about them, they are more likely to go above and beyond.

- *Make sure everyone is heard* – Efforts to ensure diversity, equity, and inclusion (DEI) have gained in importance over the past several years. Several of my clients have embraced these policies and programs to ensure DEI of thought and perspective with many of their decision-making efforts and to ensure effective feedback loops.

As you can see, there is no single best approach. Instead, there is a constant effort to know your people, to know what matters to them, and to know what motivates them.

Don't feel as if you're a failure because you don't get one-hundred-percent engagement. The reality is that some people will never engage, and in some workplaces it's more difficult to get engagement than in others for various reasons. If you get eighty percent of your workers fully engaged, you're doing great!

You Need to Engage, Too

Far too many organizations cling to the name, shame, blame, and retrain approach to "motivating" employees when undesired performance or results are observed. I put motivating in quotes because while this negative approach may quell undesired behavior, it doesn't produce the desired behavior—and it may just prompt mischievous and malevolent compliance.

Not only does this approach not work, it allows management and leadership to disengage from the issue, as in, "Well, the problem happened with Chris, so Chris is obviously to blame." Management and leadership let themselves off the hook. If they did anything wrong, they tell themselves, it was not naming, shaming, blaming, and retraining enough. In organizations with this approach, we usually find that employees wake up motivated, but it tends to be beaten out of them through the day.

The principles of human performance tell us that:

1. "People are fallible, and even the best people make mistakes.
2. Error-likely situations are predictable, manageable, and preventable.
3. Individual behavior is influenced by organizational processes and values.
4. People achieve high levels of performance because of the encouragement and reinforcement received from leaders, peers, and subordinates.
5. Events can be avoided through an understanding of the reasons mistakes occur and application of the lessons learned from past events (or errors)." [37]

This means that, just as we want workers to engage, we need the leaders to engage. They do so by accepting full responsibility for all untoward events in their organizations. How do we get leaders to do to? James Reason advises us to "substitute the individual concerned for someone else coming from the same domain of activity and possessing comparable qualifications and experience."[38] In other words, when something goes wrong, we should look first at the organizational or management systems. What might have broken down and led to this decision or action? Did we, as leaders, do something that might have contributed to this outcome?

Asking themselves first about systems, then about their leadership, should be leadership's default starting point. Even if the issue was caused by an angry employee deliberately messing up the spreadsheets, or by an over-eager worker taking on more than he was allowed to handle, that should be the starting point. Even if the problem was caused by a deranged shooter walking into their facility or a once-in-a-thousand-years earthquake, leadership should ask itself, "Did we have the proper prevention controls in place? Did we have the proper recovery mechanisms available to kick-in and quickly restore us back to pre-event?"

---

[37] Human Performance Handbook, Volume 1: Concepts and Principles. U.S. Department of Energy, DOE-HDBK-1028-2009, June 2009, pp. 1-19–1-20, https://www.standards.doe.gov/standards-documents/1000/1028-BHdbk-2009-v1/@@images/file.
[38] James Reason, *Managing the Risks of Organizational Accidents* (Burlington, VT: Ashgate, 2016), 211.

Leadership is fully engaged when it *begins* with the assumption that it owns the systems, performance, and culture within its organization. Further investigation will, we hope, pinpoint the source of the problem(s). When that happens, fully engaged leadership can take the necessary steps to prevent the thing from happening again and to better recover should it strike anyway.

Leadership that automatically blames employees is ripping its Bridge apart, destroying the Trust Truss, Culture Pillar, and more. But Leadership that steps up to grab responsibility shows that it is trustworthy and worthy of respect. It is part of the team. It is part of the Bridge, part of the quest for sustained excellence.

A Continuum

It's tempting to think of the Bridge to Excellence as being built out of various individual parts. But there are no pieces to the Bridge. It's a single entity, only divided into parts for the sake of discussion.

You must have a complete Bridge to make the journey to Sustained Excellence; you cannot ignore or forgo any piece, not even one. Removing a piece of the Bridge is like removing the violins from an orchestra, running backs from a football team, sergeants from an army, attorneys from the courtroom, chefs from the kitchen, or educators from the classroom. You may have begun your quest for excellence with a partial Bridge, but you must eventually complete and then constantly patrol your Bridge, looking for signs of wear and tear, shoring up what needs to be shored up, and rebuilding what needs to be rebuilt.

You patrol your Bridge by constantly asking yourself questions:

- What percent of the workforce actively participates and feels a sense of ownership for the organization's direction?
- What percentage of the workforce is unengaged or disengaged?
- What effect will introducing new machines, procedures, or whatever have on trust and culture?
- Will compliance get better or worse if we introduce these new rules? Have we given our leaders the skills and tools to ensure adherence to the new rules?
- Have we enabled our leaders to lead with the competencies and confidence required to bring about the necessary changes to performance and culture?
- If we go in a new direction, how do we get the culture to own and reinforce it?
- If we acquire this organization, how will it affect each of the elements of our Bridge?
- Who are our informal leaders, and are we involving them in efforts to improve?
- What should we stop doing that is either no longer adding value, disengaging, or demotivating the workforce and line leadership?
- Are we spending more time investigating our successes or our failures?

- If we have great performance and results, do we know precisely why?
- Do we have a culture that realizes continuous improvement is always possible? Is this a shared mindset?
- Are we running what-if scenarios with workers to look at possible business-continuity disrupters?
- How can we make the workplace more psychologically safe?
- How can we embrace failures and the lessons they offer?

These are just a few of the questions you must ask yourself, issues you must wrestle with. Your Bridge may seem sound, especially when your organization is producing great results. But remember that many parts of your Bridge are hidden from easy view. Quiet discontent, fear, resentment, lack of engagement, and other issues may be slowly eating into it, just as overexuberance may be knocking it slightly askew.

You, the leader, must continually patrol your Bridge, round and round, looking for signs of weakness and wear. And when you find them, you must immediately accept responsibility and work to set things right. You must be fully engaged with your Bridge.

Inexpensive Meds Will Shake Many a Bridge

There's a bridge in Turkey that was built in 850 BC, which makes it nearly 1,900 years old. According to Guinness Records, it's the oldest bridge still standing that can be dated.[39] It's a fairly simple bridge by today's standards, made of stone slabs and spanning a short distance, but it was built well. It has stood the test of time.

Your organization may have the incredibly good fortune to have built a great bridge a long time ago. Perhaps you'll be the one-in-a-million, metaphorical equivalent of the ancient bridge that still stands on its own. But don't count on it, for relying on luck is never a good strategy. And even if your bridge manages to stand on its own, it will sooner or later be marginalized as the world moves on.

I recently heard an interview with billionaire Marc Cuban. He has set up the CostPlus Drug Company to manufacture and sell medicine because, as he said, he wants to "F-up" the pharmaceutical industry. He objects to the fact that health insurance plans, third-party pharmacy benefit managers, and pharmaceutical companies have created an overly complicated system which drives prices up to the moon. This enriches them but puts the price of many medicines beyond the reach of many patients and makes the cost of care even more burdensome for the nation.

Cuban's CostPlus represents a huge potential hurricane sweeping across the pharmaceutical, insurance, and benefit manager industries. He charges, for example, $17.10 for the leukemia drug imatinib, which costs about $2,000 at standard pharmacies and $600 through some insurance plans. He sells sertraline for $3.90, compared to

---

39 "Oldest Bridge," *Guiness World Records*,
https://www.guinnessworldrecords.com/world-records/oldest-bridge.

$74 at other pharmacies. If Cuban's company survives and grows, it will blow category-5 hurricane winds across many an organization's bridge.

There's always some competitor looking to blow gale-force winds at your Bridge. And there are always new government regulations, social or economic changes, and other forces prepared to do the same.

Are you constantly inspecting and engaging with your Bridge? Are you confident it will keep standing and taking you to Sustained Excellence?

Insights from Industry Leaders

I asked leaders from a number of industries—including for-profit, non-profit, and governmental—for their insights into engagement. Specifically, I asked, Suppose you were to leave your company or position for five years and then return and your company or team is now the best at what it does. What behaviors of your people would you see that would explain why significant improvement has occurred? In other words, behaviorally, what would success and engagement look like in terms of how work is performed?

Here are some of their answers:

Tobias Read, founder, AQRA Group

- If a CEO has done their job very well, then they can hand the company seamlessly over to the next generation without interruption, and that in five years-time, the core cultural values may have evolved but are intrinsically the same.

- This does not mean that that CEO is dispensable, far from it. They probably add more hidden value than can be anticipated. But they have also built a well-functioning team and leave behind them a well-functioning company.
- By contrast, the world often sees high-profile CEOs as indispensable and brilliant leaders. However, there seems to me to be a high rate of corporate failure when those people move on, as they built a company around them, for them, and without regard to what happened when they left.

Marc Gilbertson, vice president and facility general manager, East Dubuque Nitrogen Fertilizers

- I would see zero silos and consistent and appropriate levels of intergroup communication. Folks could share concerns about problems that would not create division and would be received with the best intentions. Everyone would feel like they had a stake in the game and were valued and listened to.

Chris Boleman, president and chief executive officer, Houston Livestock Show and Rodeo

- It would be all about seeing adaptive leadership within the organization. This is the idea that the organization has stuck to its mission but has adapted the presentation based on the needs and wants to the community. If the presentation looks the same as it did when I left, then we have failed.

Jim Cusick, director of manufacturing, Shaw Industries (retired)

- There would be active signs of collaboration from floor personnel to all levels of the organization. Decisions would be pushed lower and closer to the action.

Jared Matthias, vice president of executive accounts, ChampionX

- There would be proactive behavior and empowerment to make change, change to market conditions that bring additive value props and/or reshapes our offering such that we regain an eroding margin from commoditization of our specialty. We need to evolve before we get "blockbuster'd."
- Behaviors would be consistent with feelings of empowerment, accountability, change makers and forward-looking visionary type thinker mindset.
- Work would look much more efficient, with solutions provided much faster with more accuracy and better predictiveness enabled by digital platforms managing our endless mountains of data.

Ed Senavaitis, director of corporate safety, Buckeye Partners, LP

- I would see more engagement and coaching from our leadership. I would see a workforce where incident impacts are minimized because of ownership's focus on continuous system improvements, more redundancies or fail safes in our processes, a willingness to embrace the natural fallibility of humans, and transition from a zero-incident culture to a zero-harm culture.

Joel Simon, partner, Fernelius and Simon

- Improvement would be due to people feeling like they have more ownership of the organization and the organization's culture. To me, business is inherently personal. I think of my business as a family member. Sometimes, it can be that annoying uncle at a family meal. However, if you love your organization despite its shortcomings, you can find a way to succeed.

Mike Diezi, executive director, Spec's Wine, Spirits & Finer Foods

- The best benefit of the retail brick-and-mortar business is that the guest physically visits our stores for customer service and for knowledge and expertise. The vast variety of products we carry can be best enjoyed with the proper knowledge. Learning what cigar pairs with which scotch or what glass is best to use for which wine can enhance the experience. While this information can be discovered by investing the time to research on one's own, having an expert to ask is very valuable. It is extremely beneficial to visit the stores and use the expertise of the staff. They can also suggest other ideas that may not have been apparent with online searches. These in-house teachers are happy to share their knowledge to guide our guests on their personal journeys to gain their own expertise.

  On that theme, success is always about the personal touch and relationships. This is also true with staff positions. Over the past twenty-four plus months, the entire society has met challenges, many of which were solved by remote working conditions. I believe that, in order to properly collaborate across departments and plan our ever-expanding growth, we will see our company welcome employees back to the office and have the functional departments physically officing together. Not every good idea or collaborative effort happens in a formal meeting, on an email, or during an online meeting. Some of this happens in passing in the office as ideas are informally exchanged. Some of the best ideas could come from a shy teammate that may not had been comfortable voicing their idea in a formal meeting. Also, teammates working physically closer together, according to the proximity principle, builds stronger relationships. Relationships increase communication and teamwork. Teams motivate each other to solve problems. All success circles back around to the big three of team leadership success; teamwork, communication, and maintaining that give-a-dang factor.

Key Points about Engagement

- The only way to prevent damage to your Bridge and to recover from unpreventable damage is constant diligence and vigilance.
- With respect to engagement, there are five types of employees: pioneers, "yes" people, crowd followers, skeptics, and the citizens against virtually everything (CAVE people).

- You need to understand your people, what category they fall into, and what will increase their motivation and engagement.
- If you get eighty percent of your workers fully engaged, you're doing great!
- Leadership is fully engaged when it begins with the assumption that it owns the systems, performance, and culture within its organization.
- You must have a complete Bridge to make the journey to Sustained Excellence; you cannot ignore or forgo any piece, not even one.

Questions to Consider

1. On a scale of one to ten, with one indicating you have yet to begin and ten that you are great, what score would you give for the level of engagement throughout your organization?
2. How complete is the construction of your organization's Bridge?
3. What element, if focused on, would make the biggest difference to your organization in pursuing sustainable excellence?

A Final Thought

Your organization's Bridge is not an abstract concept, checklist, or flashy thingamajig you build a model of and stick in your lobby. Always remember that regardless of your title or position, you are a leader. You are your Bridge, and your Bridge is you. From the day someone got the idea to create what became your organization, or began filling out that first piece of paperwork, or set up a folding table in the garage and began working, you have had a Bridge. You have been a Bridge.

But do you know it? Do you own it?

You can ignore your Bridge and focus on your day-to-day, quarter-to-quarter, or year-to-year matters. But that's like playing notes instead of music, shuffling instead of striding, or bunting rather than hitting a home run. Playing notes and the like may keep you alive. But it takes the ability to play beautiful music, concert after concert, to make audiences leap to their feet and demand more. That is sustained excellence! I wish you great success in building your Bridge to Excellence.

About the Author

Shawn M. Galloway is the CEO of ProAct Safety. He is a consultant, keynote speaker and author of several bestselling books on safety strategy, culture, leadership and employee engagement. Leaders have embraced his principles and teachings among the best safety-performing organizations within every major industry. He is a columnist for several magazines and one of the industry's most award-winning and recognized prolific contributors.

www.ingramcontent.com/pod-product-compliance
Lightning Source LLC
Chambersburg PA
CBHW061149220326
41599CB00025B/4413